A CANDLE
BENEATH
MY BED

A Hidden Heart

A CANDLE BENEATH MY BED

A Hidden Heart

Sandra D. Scott Johnson

ARPress
ILLUMINATING IDEAS.
EMPOWERING VOICES

ARPress
45 Dan Road Suite 5
Canton MA 02021
Hotline: 1(888) 821-0229
Fax: 1(508) 545-7580

Ordering Information:
Quantity sales. Special discounts are available on quantity purchases by corporations, associations, and others. For details, contact the publisher at the address above.

Printed in the United States of America.
ISBN-13:   Softcover   979-8-89330-799-3
                eBook   979-8-9899505-0-8
                Hardback   979-8-9899505-1-5

Library of Congress Control Number: 2024904566

CONTENTS

Dedication I

Introduction III

Chapter 1
   "Dream Lights" 1

Chapter 2
   "Upside down". 11

Chapter 3
   "Camouflage" 19

Chapter 4
   "Fiery furnace". 26

Chapter 5
   "The unfolding". 34

Chapter 6
   "Stand or fall in the mist" .40

Chapter 7
   "Running in the sun". 46

Chapter 8
   "The plans were already set". 53

Chapter 9
   "The jokester" 60

Chapter 10
   "Set it off" 65

Chapter 11
   "Life surprises". 71

Chapter 12
   "An open door" 78

Chapter 13
   "Boiling water can hurt" 85
Chapter 14
   "The unknown" 92
Chapter 15
   "Bullseye" 99
Chapter 16
   "The smell of success" 105

A CANDLE BENEATH MY BED

A Hidden Heart

Sandra D. Scott Johnson

DEDICATION PAGE

The first book, A Candle Beneath My Bed: Betrayal, was dedicated to my dear husband, Louis Johnson Sr., for all his support. Brother Joseph O. Shuman, for being that rock in our life as a big brother when we were children. That book was also dedicated to my mother, Rosa Scott, my uncle, Joseph D. Shuman, and the memory of my dear grandmother, Mary Shuman.

This book, A Candle Beneath My Bed: A Hidden Heart, is dedicated to my husband, Louis Johnson Sr., for all his support. My children-Louis Jr., Antonio, Mary, and Lashaunda. The dear memory of our mother Rosa Scott (ll-14-30 to 03-21-10); missed but not forgotten, and my grandmothers, Mary Scott and Mary Shuman.

Thank you!

INTRODUCTION

A Candle Beneath My Bed: A Hidden Heart continues the story of Jacqueline Jones' memories as a young girl facing life in Savannah, Georgia; with the combinations of fun, love, pain, drama, and strength.

When we are born, we never know what life has in store for us. God knew us before we are conceived in our mother's womb. Our life has already been planned out.

Sometimes, when young people go through things, they come out on the losing end. Family needs to be a big part of children lives especially in their family. Yes, we all have a heart, but no one can see all the pains a heart feels or when it is broken. However, God sees and knows all. There is pain in young people's lives that they deal with, which adults have no idea about.

All they can see is how that child is acting out, they just sit back and criticize them. There are so many children that are being mentally, physically, and sexually abused by family members. Believe it or not, they are also being abused by adults in the school system and are afraid to say anything, because that adult has threatened them in some way or another.

Adults need to make the children feel like they can come to them with anything. When a child or a person has been abused, their power has been taken away from them, and the abuser is in control.

With all the prayers that were going on in the family, God must have shown someone what they really needed to see. Family prayer is wonderful, but there is another important matter in a family that is needed as well. It is so good when family comes together for the family time-- to play, communicate, and pray for one another.

(A Hidden Heart)
Chapter 1

"Dream Lights"

It's a rainy afternoon, and the sound of the rain hitting the rooftop sounded like sweet melody to my ears. It sounded so good that I almost drifted off into sleep. But my mind and my body wouldn't cooperate with one another. My body says sleep, but my mind says no. So, as I lay there on my bed, I thought about all that has happened over the years, the good times, when Bill would put us inside big truck tires and rolled us around, up and down the dirt road, and we would yell out "More Bill, more!", now that was so much fun. Even if we were dizzy afterward, it didn't matter.

There were so many other wonderful things that he did for and with us as children. But now a new year is here, and this year is the beginning of a whole new set of fun and problems. The rain has stopped, and it's time to get up and move about. As I walked to our front door I took in a deep breath. The air smelled so clean and fresh, and the birds and frogs were singing their songs of praise to God. What a wonderful refreshing day that God has sent on earth! I stood there glancing outside, the flowers were so bright with colors and the greenish-colored grass seemed to come alive with a newness of life.

But there was sadness in the air that I didn't understand. As I walked around the house looking, I noticed Mom standing in the kitchen, staring out the backdoor. Her eyes were full of tears. Her facial expression indicated something was on her mind, but what was it? Suddenly, she began singing a song. The song was "when you hear of my home going, don't worry about me", that song sounded throughout the whole house. That song seemed to give Mom satisfaction.

Jackie watching her mom singing

But the song was sad to me. As I stood there for a while looking and listening to her singing, I had to ask, "Mom, why are you singing that sad song? It makes me want to cry; I don't like it."

"Well Jackie, I don't mean to make you sad, but sometimes things happen in life that make a person very sad. In some cases, it could make some individuals think about going home to be with the Lord. That is, one day, I pray you would never have to understand. Also, that you would never feel as much pain as I have in my life." Mom replied.

"On top of other things, I am having a hard time getting over Mark's death. Sometimes the memories are too much that they bring tears to my eyes. Singing brings joy to me that one day I will see him again."

"But Mom, I don't want you to die. Please don't!" I replied.

"Oh baby, I am not going anywhere now." She said with that smile that we didn't see often. "Maybe, just maybe, the baby that I am carrying now will be a boy, we will see. But I am okay, don't worry about me sweetheart." Mom said in her soft sweet voice.

I looked up at Mom and said "Mom, I am sorry that he died, but why did he die?" Mom bent over to give me a hug and spoke. "Jackie, I don't know, but it's not for me to question God."

As time passed, Mom seemed so much better. The five o'clock a.m. Sunday morning family prayer helped, not only her, but the whole family. Especially for us children, the foundation needs to be strong, because we were growing up very fast. On this day, Jerome and I were sitting on the front porch; we noticed a big truck driving down the street carrying big toys-- so, we thought. Well, that's what they looked like to us. On that same day, there were trains rolling down the tracks with different kinds of toys, as well.

As Jerome and I sat there talking, Bill walked outside, "What's going on here?" he asked. "We are sitting here looking at all those trucks carrying big toys down the street and over the railroad tracks.

Bill smiled and said, ""No those are not toys. They are rides for the big fair that comes here every year. They come on trains and big trucks like the ones you are seeing today."

"Bill, would you please take us to the fair? Please, Oh please!" I asked, jumping up and down with excitement.

"Hold on, calm down! Mama asked Stephanie and me if y'all were good, she wanted us to take y'all anyway," said Bill.

"Okay, we are always good, right Jackie?" "Oh yes, we are!"

"So, when can we go?" Jerome asked, looking up at Bill. "Saturday evening, just hold on until then."

Every night Jerome and I would stand at the back door looking at the big lights in the sky. At one point, I thought it was two big beacons in the sky for aliens that were out in space showing them the way back to their spaceship.

But the light was there to show the way to the fairground. That Friday night was another sleepless night; but sometime during that night, we drifted off to sleep. That morning, I was woken up by the sound of a train whistleblowing. I jumped up, calling out to Jerome, "Get up! It's Saturday morning. This is the day Bill and Step are going to take us to the fair!"

"I'm up. Okay, Jackie! We can't go now anyway. Bill said in the evening time that they would take us, did you forget?"

"No, I didn't. Let's do our work early, and maybe they would take us earlier." We worked so hard to finish all our chores.

It's didn't matter. We had to wait until Bill and Step were ready. Then it was time to go. As we were walking, the sound of the music and the screaming that was coming from the fairground made the suspense even more intense. As we were about to walk towards the gate, Bill told Step to take us to the back and that he would meet us there.

That's just what Step did. By the time we made it to the back, Bill was there waiting to let us in under the fence. Once we were all inside, I looked around and I was captivated by all the lights and rides.

"Let's ride!"

We just stood there looking, with my mouth wide open. "Come on Jackie, let's get on some rides!" said Jerome with a look of pure pleasure on his face. We rode on many rides, ate corn dogs, popcorn, and drank sodas. This was the beginning of a yearly enjoyment day with Bill and Step; for many years to come. The best night of our life.

Another thing to look forward to is being at our family gathering-- it was also one of the happiest times of the month. Grandma May still has family dinner every 3rd Sunday.

Collard greens with smoke neck bones, rice, macaroni and cheese, potato salad, baked ham, cakes, pies and so much more. With all that food, it seemed like they cooked all day. Oh, let's not forget the fried chicken, which was the best thing on the table.

The process of getting those chickens prepared was still amazing, and the preparation was the same as before. The two weeks cleaning out, the chopping off the head, soaking in hot water, plucking off the feathers, burning off the extra fine feathers over the fire, cleaning, washing, and getting them ready to the frying pan.

It was still sad to see those poor chickens jumping over the ground. "I wonder if they feel any pain?" I don't record them making a sound., but once the chicken was on the table looking so... good, you forgot all about how they got there. And they tasted, so... good!

As the adults sat around the table talking and laughing with each other during and after the meal, it was great family time. The way the adults act toward each other, teaches the younger ones how they shall get along with one another. If there were issues between them, we children never knew about it. After the meal was over, all the ladies came together, and they worked hard cleaning up.

After the cleaning, Mom and Aunt Betty were standing in the corner of the room talking; it seems to be very important, going by the looks on their faces. That may be the reason, why on the following day, Mom told us that we were going to move again. It seems like out of nowhere Mom was able to find a nice four-room house that looked so much better than all the other houses that we had lived in, if that is what they were talking about, Great!

"Moving out"

This house had plum trees and a big mulberry tree in the backyard. There was no doubt that Mom worked hard to make things better for her family. It was shown in everything she did. I, along with my sibling didn't understand how she did it, but she did.

After walking home from the bus stop about two miles away, she put her feeling aside to make her family happy. The good thing was that we were still surrounded by other family members.

Wow! we were so happy that we were moving up in the world. There was still no indoor plumbing, but the new house had electricity. What a joy now, especially when someone blessed us with a black-and-white television. To add color, all we did was find some clear colored wrapping paper to cover it, and Hah! We had a colored television.

As a family that made us very happy, and, as children, we had nothing to worry about. We didn't have to work. All we had to do was enjoy life and enjoy being children. One of the adults in our neighborhood said she was tired of walking home from the bus stop that was so far from her home.   So, they all came up with an idea to get together and go house to house knocking on doors, getting people to sign their names on a petition for the bus to come across the railroad track.

They took along all the children that were old enough to help. When people stand together, a lot can be done. With all the hard work we did, the bus was finally able to come our way, and one of the stops were in front of Grandma May's house. Oh, what fun it was riding on the bus with Mom going downtown to buy us new shoes and clothes for special occasions; like Christmas, Easter, and Back-to-school.

There were times when she took Step and me downtown to get our hair done. We don't know how Mom did it, but she did everything she can do to make sure we have a wonderful childhood. But sometimes things don't always go as planned.

There came a storm out of nowhere that caused a change in my life and took on a whole new meaning of happiness. The summer was over, and the cold weather was setting in. There was a great joy that I felt on the inside because tomorrow is the day that I have been waiting for so long -- my thirteenth birthday.

I would be a teenager headed towards adulthood. What a joy it would be! I was thinking that my life would be a joyful journey when I become a teen. I couldn't wait.

Three more years, then I would be already eligible to date. This is what teenage girls look forward to. I started making fantasy plans for my thirteenth birthday party. Although I knew we didn't have any money, but it doesn't hurt to dream.

As I lay there on my bed listening to the night sounds of the whooping birds and the trains rolling down the tracks, they were more beautiful than ever. I drifted off into a night of sweet dreams and fantasies.

"Wake up child, it's only a Dream!"

Then the morning light and the sounds of the rooster crowing woke me up, out of a dream of pure fun and laugher. It was a great dream! As I sat up in my bed, looking around, "Oh, it is a lovely day!" I said to myself.

But now the dream was over and real life was about to hit me head-on. My expectation of a joyful teen life was shattered quicker than someone who threw a baseball to a window on a hot summer day. Here I was, thinking that a child's life should be a great time of joy. Spending time with your family and friends shall be a happy time.

But now it's four months into my thirteenth birthday and I was so happy to finally be a teenager. But evidently, life is not always what you dream it should be. The thing about dreams is that, sooner or later, you will wake up and face the real world. Mom was expecting another baby, and it was almost time for her to deliver. Something I wasn't looking forward to.

I was the baby girl and I wanted it to remain that way. I started wishing that it would be a boy. But when two weeks passed, Mom delivered a baby girl. Her name was Katrina. At first, I didn't want to see the baby at all. But after a day, I walked into the room to look at that tiny baby laying there on her bed, wondering what happens to her eyes. "Hey Jerome, come here!" I called out.

"What do you want, Jackie?" He replied.

"What happens to this baby's eyes? Why they are not green like Tim's?" I asked. "I don't know, let's ask Step. She might know why." Step was sitting there in the living room doing her crossword puzzle as always. Then we both ran in, "Step!" Jerome and I called out at the same time.

"Hey, slow down!" said Step. "We want to ask you something." "What?" she responded.

"What is wrong with that baby's eyes? They are not green like Tim's."

"There is nothing wrong with her eyes. All babies' eyes are not the same color. Sometimes, we pick up things from past generations. Things like skin tone, eye color, height, or habits; that's why Tim's eyes are different from ours." Step explained. "Oh, okay." Jerome replied.

"Well, that's okay. She is pretty anyway." Jerome said as he ran out of the room.

One good thing about the baby is that Mom is home now, and it was so great having her home with the family. Even though it was only for a few weeks, the time passes quickly, before we realized it was time for her to go back to work. Jerome and I stayed at home while Katrina and Tim stayed at Grandma May's house during Mom's work hours.

Step would come over and stay with us, but for some reason, this day she didn't.

"Katrina in the arms of safety"

CHAPTER 2

"Upside down"

This was the day that my life took a turn that would affect the rest of my life. It was a lovely day as Jerome, and I sat playing tic-tack-toe. "Jackie, I won again!" said Jerome. "Boy, I let you win," I responded. As we went back and forth about who was the best, a call was heard. "Jerome!" Dad called out.

"Yes Sir," Jerome responded.

"I need you to go to the store for me. Put on a jacket, it's cold outside." The store was about a mile away from the house. "Okay, Dad, what do you want from the store? Can Jackie go with me?", replied Jerome. "No, Jackie needs to stay and wash the dishes. You go and hurry back. Come here and get the money and the list of things I want you to buy for me.

As Jerome walked in the room for the money and the list of items Dad wanted from the store, Dad told him to "Watch out for cars,". "Hey, Jackie. I'll be back, and don't you cheat on that game." "Oh boy, I won't cheat. I'll wait until you get back." I responded back. While Jerome was on his way to the store, I washed a few dishes and went back to my room. But within a minute, Dad called me. "Jackie, come here."

"Yes sir, where are you?" I asked.

"In my bedroom", he replied. As I walked to that room, I felt so uncomfortable. "Come here, sit down". My knees started to tremble.

"Come on, all I want to do is talk to you. Don't be afraid," Dad said. With those words, I slowly sat down beside him. But something was wrong; Dad started to move closer and closer toward me. My heart began to beat heavily as if it was about to come out of my chest.

The smell of that alcohol filled the air. Yes, he has been drinking. He began talking to me about how I was getting older and one day he knows that I would start dating a young man. The more he talked, the closer he got. I felt as though I was suffocating.

But then, he did something that I know a real father should never do. He began touching me in an inappropriate way that no father should ever touch his child. "No! Stop Daddy! What are you doing? Please stop, don't do this! I don't like this!" But he continued his abusive and destructive treatment towards me, his very own child! Then I cried out uncontrollably. "No ......! No ! Stop!"

I began wondering in my mind, what is this man thinking. "My God! Here I am, a thirteen-year-old and my father is sexually assaulting me." Anger couldn't even begin to describe the hate that was setting in, like a winter storm that came out of nowhere--and that storm won't go away.

In my mind I was thinking, if only a knife was lying around, this would have been his last day on earth. "I am a child!" Over and over in my head, I said it. "I am a child! Lord, I am a child!" His drinking does not justify his behavior. The smell of that alcohol and what he did was more than sickening, it made me sick to my stomach!

That smell would be in my mind forever. There should never be enough alcohol in the world to make a father do what he did to his own child. All I could do was cry. "Jackie, you stop that crying now!" He said in an angry tone. At that time, he realized that he couldn't achieve his goal.

He looked at me and yelled. "Just get out of here now! If you tell anyone, I will beat you to the point you will wish that you were dead, do you understand me? Now, get out!" this man said. My father, yes, my father looked at me as though he hated the ground I walked on. Well, for what he did, he sure didn't love me.

I thought to myself, he can beat me all he wants, even to the point of death, but that would not even come close to what he has already done. I jumped up and ran straight to my bedroom. As I sat there in the corner of my room, my head hanging in shame. All the joy of my thirteenth birthday was taken away from me at that moment, and all I did was sit there in disgrace.

As tears rolled down my face, I was wondering what was taking Jerome so long, it seemed like he was gone forever. But then I heard the front door opening. I picked up a book and pretended that I was reading it. Then there was a knock at my room door.

"A mask of disgrace"

"Who is it?" I asked, but I knew who it was. "Jackie, it's me girl let me in." "Hold on, come in," I reluctantly answered him. I stopped crying and sat up. Jerome walked into the room. "What are you doing, Jackie?"

"Just sitting here reading this book," I replied. Jerome was my brother and best friend, and I couldn't tell him anything.

I couldn't tell him about what happened to me. Therefore, I tried to look as though nothing was wrong, by looking at the book. "Jackie, what is wrong with you? You look like you were crying, and you look so sad. Since when did you started reading a book upside down?" He asked me in a concern tone. Jerome knew something was wrong, but he didn't know what.

At that moment I wanted to run into my brother's arms and just cry, and cry and tell him all that happened while he was gone, but I couldn't. Before he left to go to the store, I was happy. "Jerome, do you mind if I lay down for a while? I'm so sleepy." I replied. But I wasn't sleepy at all, I just wanted to be left alone.

"Okay, Jackie, I'll see you later." As I sat there in my room alone, I started wondering what I should do. "I know what I'll do, maybe I'll run away, or I'll just kill myself. No one will miss me." Those words went over and over in my mind. What kind of love is this? This man said he loved us. If this is love, I wonder what he calls hate. He doesn't love me! He hates me! But why?"

As I sit in my room and thought these things to myself, I just put a pillow over my mouth as I screamed out in so much pain. I couldn't stop my tears from falling. What a very sad state of mind I was in. Here I am, only thirteen, with my whole life in front of me. What kind of life it would be for me now? God only knows. That day, I stopped living. And that was the day I died inside. I was walking around-- building up hate for my father day after day.

I began acting out, showing that I was suffering inside. Anyway, I knew how-- fighting in school so many times, hoping that someone would notice that something was wrong with me; but no one did. Well, one day after many attempts, my school class was on their way from lunch and the teacher told us to go to the bathroom before going to our classroom.

As I waited in line, a classmate came in running, "Jackie! Come quickly, your brother is fighting!" "What! Oh, no!" Before I knew it, I rushed in and pushed Jerome out of the way.   And I took over. I grabbed that boy by the neck and squeezed as hard as I could. As I held on, I repeated, "Don't you ever, ever, touch my brother again. Do you hear me? Do you?" I screamed as I squeezed, I forgot all about going to the bathroom.

"Jackie! No!" the teacher was yelling and pulling me at the same time. "Stop, get off of him! When I finally snapped out of it and looked around, everybody's mouth was wide open. "Jackie, you need to go to the principal's office, NOW!" The teacher said in an upset voice.

"Why me? What about him? He jumped on my brother, and no one, no one hits my brother! Not if I am around." I responded in a very angry tone. "Jackie, I'm speechless. If I ever had to hit you, I must pick up a chair and throw at you. Why are you so angry, young lady?" My teacher said.

As I walked out of the classroom and headed to the principal's office, I was wondering what is going to happen to me. But it didn't matter, if everyone knew who I was and never touch my brother again, it was worth it. Oh yes, I was suspended for a few days and that was okay. Everybody was afraid of me after that day, and no one ever bothered Jerome again.

Sometimes, when bad things happen to your life, it causes you to go inside a shell. You must keep moving, or else it would take over and you will be no better than the one that caused the pain. I always found great comfort climbing and sitting up in Grandma May's chaining-berries tree. That was my world-- where no one could harm me.

There was a lot going on around me, but the Lord kept my mind intact. He always had my future in His hands. I wasn't in control of anything. It was in His hand. As a child I always enjoyed writing short stories and poetry, but what gave me even more pleasure was running track in school. Just feeling the wind hitting my face gave me great joy. I always loved running, so at school, I ran track and did other activities which gave me some peace within. Working in the school library, helping my schoolmates checking books in and out was something that gave me great joy.

Going to middle school was a great place. But I was all alone. I felt so sad inside, and no one cared about me. But I did learn a lot about cooking and sewing. Frying and stewing chicken were my favorite. Whenever I learned something new, I would try it out at home. Our Mom was always getting on me about messing up her food. But after a while, they loved my cooking.

But for some reason, my little covered-up joy didn't last long. Middle school was a great place of learning, but it was also another difficult time for me. I found out that some of the things that gave me so much joy, also can turn into a nightmare. There are all kinds of people in this world. As you walk through life, people are watching you. They watch and study you for weeks, even months before they make a move. It's like a lion waiting and watching for that weakest animal in the herd, and when the time is just right, he or she attacks.

Currently, I was that weak animal, and I didn't know that a wild animal was watching me around the school. Until this day, while working in a small room wheresome library books are kept, someone walked in, closed the door, and turned off the lights. "Who's in here?" I asked as I felt for the light switch to tum the lights back on.

But the person wouldn't say anything. They just grabbed me and tried kissing me. I fought back and yelled, then he spoke, and I recognized the voice. "Mr. Peabody! What are you doing? Please stop!" I demanded, as tears rolled down my face. Flashback about my Dad went through my mind. The school principal is now trying to sexually abuse me too. What's next? He didn't go near as far as my Dad, but the idea of him even trying to kiss and hold me was more than I could even bear. I began biting him and trying to find my way to the light switch.

He held my hands; he was so much bigger and stronger than me. It seemed like I wasn't getting anywhere, so, I cried, bit him, and begged him to please let me go. I screamed and he covered my mouth with his hand. I put up a fight in that small room that day.

He realized that I was fighting with everything I had in me. A kick in the right spot at the right time dropped him to his knees. I walked out and hid in the girl's bathroom for a few minutes. "When will the tears stop." I thought to myself.

"Stop screaming"

That was my last day working in any library. Now here is more pain I must deal with. To this day, I can't deal with anyone holding me and I have to fight to get free, even if playing only. In the evening after school, I have seen this man ride up and down our street. Once I knew what type of car he had, whenever I noticed his car or any car that looks like his--coming down or up the road, I would run into the house and hide. Should this be a life for a child?

No, young girl. No one should have to live their life like this, a life of fear. I didn't feel like I had anyone in this world to talk to, so I kept it all inside. Living in a shell hiding behind a mask is now my way of life. I should have been able to enjoy my teen years. A lot of joy had been taken from me. There was no safety at home or at school.

"Can you see me"

CHAPTER 3

"Camouflage"

Men and women have big problems when they abuse children. They need help. If they can only understand what they have done to that child. Well, to me, I don't think they would really care anyway. As time passed, those dirty dark secrets were tearing me apart inside. I hated myself. Why should I care when no one else did. But eventually, I learned how to hurt my feelings well.

But there wasn't anything I could have done about it anyway. It seemed like things in life were trying very hard to kill me at a very early age or mess my mind up. But I guess God saw that, and I can handle it. Mom seems to love the Lord with all her heart. But I wondered, did the Lord let her in on that dark secret?

Well, if He did, I don't think I will ever know. Besides, Mom had her own problems to deal with--like that man she calls her husband. On this Tuesday night, as before Mom wanted to go to church, she decided to ask Dad. His responses were "NO! You won't be going anywhere tonight. Now you go in there and bring me something to drink."

"Okay Matt, but I really want to go." Mom said in a sad voice. Well, before I could blink my eyes, that man we called dad hit Mom so hard that it knocked her to the floor. Then he turned around, headed toward his dresser as if he was about to get something out of his drawer. Mom knew what was about to happen. She cried out, "Bill, get the kids out of here!" Another night of him being intoxicated with alcohol. People like this don't need a family because they don't know how to love and treat them the way they should be.

We had no idea what Dad was about to do to our Mom. Bill noticed what was going on. He ran in and knocked Dad to the floor and kicked him in the stomach. Afterward, he grabbed him around the neck and Bill was saying words that we never heard before. Mom called out to Bill; *DON'T KILL HIM BILL, LET HIM GO!*

In my mind, I was saying "WHAT! KILL HIM BILL DO IT, DO IT NOW!" But Bill stopped because it seems to upset Mom so much. We stood by crying for our mother not knowing what was happening. Mom called out "Kids go to your grandmother's house, now! Run! Go now!" We all ran as fast as we could.

If Bill didn't do what he did, our Mom wouldn't have escaped that night with her life. So, he did what he had to do to keep that from happening. Bill told us when he was younger he watched Dad beat our mom sometimes day and night but he was too young to do anything about it but, not anymore, it stops here tonight!

Mom was able to get away, and we all ran to Grandma May's house. Uncle Pete looked at us and asked what was wrong. After telling them all that went on, he called his other brothers. All of Mom's brothers that lived in the neighborhood came running to the house, but Dad was already gone. They were so upset that they all went looking for Dad. They looked for hours but couldn't find him. A few days later, Mom called Bill over to have a talk with him.

Her response was, "Son, thank you for saving me; but I don't want you to worry about it. I don't want you to lose your freedom because of Matt." She also said that she believes, 'God will work things out one day'.

None of us couldn't understand what Mom was talking about. Was Bill supposed to stand by and watch Dad kill her? No! That wasn't going to happen, not this night or any other nights. Mom was all that we had. Later, Mom was cleaning out the dresser drawer, and she found out that Dad had in it was a small tranquiller gun. "Wow! Was that what he was planning on using on Mom to make sure she wouldn't make it to church that night?" I thought to myself.

I didn't understand why Dad was so angry with the world; but he was and with everyone that was in it. It appears Dad was always mad about something. The only way he dealt with it was to take it out on the ones that were close by. Days went by before anyone heard from him.

Bill was tired of seeing our mother beaten just because she wanted to go to church. After a while, Bill felt bad about what he did, so he just stayed away more and more. We all missed having Bill around. He started working and he also met a young lady by the name of Pam Robertson. I felt that he had abandoned us. He was our protector and now that he wasn't around anymore, other things were going wrong.

One day he finally came home, but he wasn't alone. Now a face could finally be put with the name Bill often talked about. This was the first time we met her. It was nice to see how happy she seemed to be with Bill. Two months passed; Bill came back to the house. This time he rode up in his new car, at five o'clock on a Saturday evening.

He was with that same beautiful young lady. And when she smiled, she was even more beautiful. Bill said, with a big grin on his face, "Family, I want you to know that Pam is my wife now. We got married yesterday." Mom wasn't surprised; they both seemed to love one another. I understood that our big brother was in love, and that he must live his own life, besides, we liked Pam.

One thing I knew, if he had any idea what was going on, he would have killed that man we call daddy, without even thinking. So, I guess-- him not knowing was a blessing in disguise. I didn't want him to lose his freedom, not at all. There are no doubts whether Bill loved us. We knew he did; he proved it so many times. We can say that our big brother was a real man.

That day Bill left us for a life of his own, I was sad and happy at the same time. Sad to see him go, but happy that he met someone. Then, after saying my goodbye, I turned around and walked into the house, hoping that he would have a great life. We will just remember all the good times with our big brother, and there will never be another like him.

Now, I am much focus on Katrina growing up. My little brother, Tim, is doing great as well.

Getting into everything he can and trying things that he shouldn't, but it's fun playing and being around him. He is so handsome. Katrina had it made, so it seems everyone just loved her.

I loved her as well. But I couldn't help worrying about her protection from Dad. "What if, what happened to me happened to Katrina as well? "OH NO! I need to figure out how to protect her and look out for her, because Dad is an evil man". I thought to myself.

As Katrina was getting older, I watched her day and night when she was around, and kept the reasons why to myself. I was so afraid that our Dad would try his act again, but this time-- with Katrina. What on earth would I do?" I thought to myself. That question was always on my mind. The only thing I could do for now was watch, pray and hope that God was not angry with me, and He would answer my prayers.

There was a time when I wondered if our mother had any idea what kind of man she had married and the danger she was putting her girls in. My God! Did she have any idea about me at all? By this time, Katrina was three years old. It was time for Dad to show off his children again. He got so much pleasure when other people gave him compliments about how well his children behave.

He also knew that each time he would take us anywhere, someone would always give us some money. This was a way for him to get extra money for himself to buy a drink of alcohol. Well, the truth is, it seems like he was only using his children for his own gain.

The only thing he wanted was the money for himself. Now that the visiting is over, it's time to go home. Walking home at night wasn't always scary-- there were some good times too. But this night, as we were walking, Katrina was sitting on Dad's shoulder, Jerome and I were walking, holding Tim's hand.

"Jerome," called Dad. "Come get Katrina and take Tim, and walk ahead. I need to talk to Jackie about something." He spoke. As Jerome did as he was told, my mind began to wonder what Dad was up to now.

I didn't want Jerome to leave me, because if he was around, I felt safe. But as Jerome did as he was told and walked, he looked straight ahead. "Why won't he look back? " I thought to myself. At that moment, Dad reached over to touch me on the chest. This time, with everything in me I slapped his hand away.

I started running as fast as I could. As I passed Jerome, he yelled out. "Jackie! Wait, okay. I see that you want to race. But I can't. I have Tim and Katrina!" Jerome yelled out. Well, racing wasn't on my mind at all. All I wanted was to get home and sit in my room, that old favorite place-- the corner.

As I raced home, tears were streaming down the sides of my face. I began questioning God. "Lord, why is this happening again? Why?" Without stopping, I ran straight to my room. I sat in that same corner that I had sat in before. I began to pray, not knowing how to, but I was hoping that God will hear me anyway.

"Lord, I don't understand what is going on. What is wrong with me? Why doesn't my father love me? Why?" As I cried, I covered my mouth so Mom wouldn't hear me. "What have I done to deserve this? Please show me. I don't want to live anymore, Lord! I just want to die. Please take me out of this mess, please!" This was my prayer. I was praying and crying at the same time.

To me, I was thinking that dying would be so much better than living. Then my mind went back to that snake bite. I was wondering to myself; was this some type of pay back for what he did in order to save my life?

Well, if so, I would have been better off dead. That love I had for my father was gone. This scar will last for life. I wondered to myself whether he understood what he had done to me.

My life will never be the same anymore. But one thing I didn't know was that, the Lord saw everything that I was going through. There was a light that I couldn't see, because of all the pain in my life. But I believed that God did see and answered my prayer that night because after that, he never tried touching me inappropriately again.

A HEART

*"I have a heart... Can you see it? Can you hear it beat?
Can you feel it? It plumps the blood of life that flows
through my veins, but there's no way you can see the
pains."*

*"It's covered with layers of skin and muscles, but
God sees it. Yes, it may be hidden from man, but GOD
knows just what my heart can stand."*

*"There is no age for pain when we are born, and that
first breath of air is inhaled, it is our step in the world
of misbelief, but as times pass you will see God's plans
come together and soon some happiness will be gained."*

"The tears of a heart"

Hello, world! This is a great day. Waking up by the train and rooster is always great, but there is a bitter coldness outside this morning. I can't seem to get up. Mom always remembers to have the house warm for us and this morning is no exception. The house is warm but there is a chill that goes through my bones.

Then I remembered, Wow! Today is my fourteenth birthday. My mind went back to my thirteenth birthday. I was so terrified thinking that it might repeat itself. So, I was watching and ready for anything that was coming my way. I knew that God was moving on my behalf and that he was not angry with me. So now if anyone tried to hard me in any way, I was going to do my best to make sure that would be a day they would never forget as long as they live.

On this birthday, I found out that Uncle John's birthday was the same date as my birthday. The family came together and gave him a very nice family dinner. Because my birthday was on the same date, the family gave me a cake and some ice cream. That day, I felt so wonderfully loved. At this time, I was so happy to have a birthday that brought a big happy smile to my face. That was a great birthday to remember.

CHAPTER 4

"Fiery furnace"

The family prayer is still going on and we are going to church. Today I am feeling better; although we didn't have a car, our uncles made sure that the whole family had a way to get to church. It was a very cold morning-- ice hanging from the house and the trees, and the ground was slippery because of the ice. But it didn't matter because it was a very happy time. It is a few days before Christmas. All of us are on the Christmas program.

Besides all the gifts that was under the tree Mom surprised me by allowing me to wear nylon stockings for the very first time. They felt so strange on my legs. "Step, my legs are cold, and they feel funny!" I called out to my big sister. "I know. When I started wearing them, they felt that way to me too, but the more you wear them, you would get to love them," Step responded.

As I sat there in church, I just couldn't keep my hands off my legs. I was so busy paying attention to my legs that I didn't hear them when they called my name to say my part on the program. Jerome was sitting beside me, so he gave me a nudge in my side with his elbow. "Jackie! They're calling your name."

"Oh, here!" raising my hand like we do in school. "Girl, what's wrong with you? We are not in school!" Jerome whispered as the other children giggled softly on their seats.

"You children stop that; you are not outside!" said one of the mothers of the church. Going to church was one of the fun things in our life. One reason why was you never knew what was going to happen. Just being there watching the saints praise the Lord was a memorable occasion. Although, we as children didn't understand what was going on.

Some of them looked funny in the way they were moving and jumping up and down. It reminded me of the chickens when they were being prepared for dinner on a Saturday evening. Jumping and moving all around, but the difference between them and the chickens was that tears were running down their faces.

"What's wrong with them?"

There were so many times when it became so scary. Especially when we had to just sit there watching the preachers pray for people that were possessed by demons. It was a scary thing for us as children when those demons started talking back. Wow!

It would say things like, 'I'm not coming out', and started laughing. Well, at this point, some of us ran and crawled under the long benches in the church. But those spiritually strong preachers began to pray the 'prayer of faith' and cast all those demons out. Afterward, those people started praising the Lord. They were so happy, and so were we.

They were so busy praying for the people; we as children didn't think they realized how frightened we were. But they did. One of the missionaries talked with us and tried to explain what was going on. It helped some, but not much. After that, there were times some of those same preachers came from New York to run revivals. They would stay with Grandma May, Uncle Pete, and Aunt Betty.

We, as children, noticed them walking outside, we would run and hide because to us they looked like walking angels. We weren't sure what would happen, so we got out of their way. I'm pretty sure they seen us and smile.

What is wrong now? Why that same power is not in the churches today anymore? Maybe because, the bible says, these come through fasting and praying. Are the preachers eating too much and not praying as they should? That's something to wonder about.

Pastoral Sunday—it was the best time at church. The sisters would cook some of the best-tasting food in the world. After church, they would set the food up on a long table with white tablecloths and serve everyone outside in the church backyard. They didn't give us a small amount of food just because we were children. Oh no! Our plates were so heavy with all kinds of food. Churching was good but the food was great!

"Come on let's eat"

Church, eat, smile, and hide-- you can only do so much at a time, but the real pains of life were forever present. After going through so many things as a child, I begin thinking this is how life was supposed to be. Aside from the bad experiences I had with my father, I had to deal with mental abuse as well. That was the first time I ever noticed prejudices; and it was coming from some of the people around me— even some of my family members.

I couldn't understand why some people could be so mean towards other people. They say things that can cut deep inside the heart. If God made you the way he wants you to be, why should you try to change to please others? There are all kinds of people with different shades of color, that make up this wonderful world that we live in.

When a grown-up in the family makes fun of a person because of your complexion, that's sad. I was a very light - skinned girl with red hair. So, I thought to myself, "Maybe if I stay outside in the sun, I will become darker. And maybe they will like me better." I worked so hard at it just so they wouldn't tease me anymore.

I asked our mom, "Why was my hair so red?" She responded, "Honey, it's all in God's plan, but maybe I can do something to turn it darker, would you like that?" With a smile on my face, I replied "Oh yes ma'am I would!" So, each time mom would wash my hair; I don't know what she used but my hair began to turn darker. That made me feel so much better.

Well, I thought one problem was resolved but here is another one. Because on the other side was my father' s family. Grandma Sharon Jones, after Dad and Mom moved out, Dad didn't go around her very much, but Mom did as often as possible. When we were older, Mom would drop us off for the weekend stay. On this weekend, Jerome and I stayed with Grandma Sharon. At first, it was scary; we would sit on her stairs crying for a very long time.

Standing and looking out of the window, hoping that Mom would turn back, see us crying and come pick us up. But, she didn't. Grandma Sharon was a very nice person, and she loved us. She hugged us and talked with us; and that made us feel so much better. "Come here! I have something for you both." She said with a smile on her face. There were all kinds of toys on the table that she had pick up from other children who were playing and have left their toys in her yard.

Jerome and I were feeling at home by now. A few hours passed, then Grandma Sharon called us to the table for dinner. The food was so good! Both of our grandmothers knew how to cook, the foods tasted so good. After dinner, we cleaned up the kitchen.

"Jackie, come here, it's bedtime. But before bed, you both need to take a bath. Jackie, you go first. Your water is ready", She said. "Okay thank you Grandma." But just as I stepped in, I yelled out, "Ouch! Grandma, it's too hot and it smells like bleach."

"I know that. Sit in the tub. It's not that bad. I will bring you something to wash with", she said. When I looked up, Grandma Sharon had a big scrubbing brush. "Let me help you", as she started to scrub my body with that brush. It was hurting me, but I was too afraid to say anything. As Grandma Sharon was scrubbing, she repeatedly say, "Jackie, I don't want to ever see your complexion looking like this anymore.

You're not supposed to be this dark! I think, if you stay here in the house this weekend out of the sun, your complexion may clear up a little," She said in a gentle and sweet tone. Although her voice wasn't harsh, I couldn't help wondering if Grandma thought that we didn't take baths. But we did. We may not have a bathtub like hers, but we use Mom's washtub that she uses to wash our clothes. Mom made sure of that.

But that wasn't so bad; it was other things and other words that played over and over in my head day and night. Some words that someone said to me on my mother's side was, 'Jackie, you will never be anything in life', 'You're going to be just like your no-good drunken father'. Those words made me feel so bad about myself. I started thinking that something was wrong with me. But what was it?

They would say things and laugh about it. I lived with my dad and I knew how he was. "Why would they say that to me?" I asked myself. We all have feelings-- children as well as adults. You should never put anyone down in order to make yourself feel better. That day, they gave me something that they didn't realize. Yes, my spirit was broken. Oh yes it was! So now, I was that bad girl looking to hurt anyone who crosses me.

If you cross me you will pay, if you cross my brothers and sisters, you will pay!' I will hurt you before you hurt me' was my goal now. My name was around the school and our neighborhood, that if you start a fight with me, I would finish and win it. I don't care if they are boys or girls. But as time passed, I realize that just because they said it, I will not be what they said I would be; but better, and they will see.

The opportunity for me to prove to myself that I was not what they said I was or what they said I would be was not easy. We as children were taught that we shall always have respect for adults. But the question is, *why don't they respect us as children?*

Is it because we are just children? If so, children have feelings too. "Does anyone have any knowledge of a damaged child? *Can't they see her or his pains?"* I prayed that the Lord would let someone see the pain in my eyes that leads to my heart.

Grandma May was a praying woman, and maybe she did see something. She would pray and read the bible to us everyday. Being at her house was a place of peace and safety.

Grandma Sharon was a different woman altogether. I believe that there are no other women in this world like our Grandma Sharon. She was a very short, strong-willed woman, and she didn't back down from anyone. Not even a man, ah......... maybe, just maybe, I have been blessed with some of her characteristics when it came to standing up for my right. She is from the tribe of the Navaho Indians, a people who is known for being strong warriors. One day we were outside playing and there was a man that drank too much.

Grandma Sharon asked him in a very nice voice, "Would you please leave from around her door with his disgusting language;" she told him that her grandchildren are outside playing. She also said she don't like the way he is verbally expressing himself, especially in front of us, besides he was drunk!" Well, he decided that he wanted to act up even more so. Calling her all kinds of names we as children have never heard of before.

This was making her more and more upset. She kindly told him, "I Warned you two times sir already, and after the third warning, I will go in my house, and you wouldn't like what I have when I come back out. So, leave and leave now!" Well, maybe he thought she was kidding around with him.

"Okay, you will regret this day for the rest of your life!" she told him; with those words, she turned around and walked in her house. Grandma Sharon came back with a pot in her hand. "Jackie, you and Jerome take the other kids in the house now! And close the door," Grandma said.

"Didn't I tell you to leave"

Before we could get in the house and close the door, Grandma took that big of whatever was in it and threw it on that poor man. That man hit the ground kicking and screaming. "Oh, lady what was that!! AH OH GOD HELP ME! IT BURNS!! Ouch! Ouch! Help somebody please help me ouch.................... I'm so sorry!" The man screamed as he rolled over and over on the ground.

With that man screaming so loud, dad ran to see what was going on. "What is going on out here? And what is wrong with that man screaming like that?" dad asked. "Well, I threw a big pot of potash and bleach on him!" Grandma replied.

"Oh my god mama what have you done?" Rushing toward the water hose, he turned the water on and began wetting him down. With all that commotion, the people across the street saw what was happening and called the police as well as the ambulance.

That man looked like he had been cooked alive. With our mouths open and our eyes stretched wide open with the other children stood there looking on. "Jackie, take those children back in the house and you stay there too, and don't come back out here," dad said. It took about one hour before the police showed up with the ambulance, so it seems. But it was only a few minutes. This was the most excitement we had ever seen.

"What happened?" asked the police, as the ambulance medical staff worked on the injured man. "Sir, it was self-defense. I had to protect myself and my grandchildren. That man was acting crazy. I was afraid. I begged him to leave, but he wouldn't. He was acting as if he wanted to hurt us. I wasn't going to let that happen, especially not to my grandchildren," Grandma Sharon told the police.

After working on him for about ten minutes, he was taken to the hospital for treatment. The police continued to question grandma about the incident. "Mss. Jones, why didn't you call the police after the man wouldn't leave you alone?"

"Well sir, for one reason I don't have a phone, and I called the police before from my neighbor's house about this same man, when he acted up before. It took two long…. hours before someone showed up. He could have killed someone by then. And the way he was carrying on this time I wasn't taking any chances, not this time, no sir! Not this time," she replied.

"Well Ms. Jones, I would put this in my report. Now Mr. Williams may press charges against you when he gets better. I'm not sure, you will have to wait and see. Please don't leave town," said the police officer. "Okay, but where am I going? I'll be here.", Grandma replied.

CHAPTER 5

"The unfolding"

After six months passed, Grandma still hadn't heard anything else concerning that incident. It was as if nothing had happened. I hope that the man didn't die. But after that day people, especially men respected her, to the point they seem to be somewhat afraid of her. Grandmamma Sharon moved into another apartment. This one was upstairs as well, the grands loved it as much as she did.

Although she was short in stature and didn't allow anyone to walk over her, she was a gentle, loving, and beautiful person. She has talents that many people wished they had. She especially loved her grandchildren to the point where she'd pick out who we should or shouldn't play with.

All of us as grandchildren felt safe around her. But that's what grandparents should do, help keep the children safe, and give them that extra love and care that they sometimes feel that they weren't getting from home. The weekends at her house became our fun time away from home. We started looking forward to going there.

Sleeping in her bed felt very comforting.   It seems to make all the pains in life disappeared. Yes, there was a big difference between her and Grandma May.

Grandma May was a more serious and spiritual person. Grandma Sharon was a person with her own special qualities. We also attended her church services as well. It was so different from what we were used to. But it was nice to see that there are churches of all kinds.

I can recall many times Grandma Sharon playing dodge ball with us. Although she was an adult and our grandmother, she didn't think that she was too old to play with us. Taking us to the park was such an enjoyable time, but what we loved best was when she would walk us to the store and tell us to get anything we wanted, no matter how much it cost.

There were a few things both grandmothers had in common, and one was that they both had peach trees with the best tasting peaches ever, and the other was that they both loved their grandchildren. Going to Grandma Sharon's, me and my other siblings were always prepared for the unexpected. We loved the toys, money, candies, and those great tasting meals, ah... ah... so good, all that was great with us.

There were even times when some of the children in her neighborhood tried to pick fights with us. But by the time Grandma was done with them we never, never had to worry about that again. Grandma Sharon was getting older. But it seemed like her age didn't slow her down, not at all. She said that she was going to enjoy her life to the fullness.

Well, even though it wasn't the weekend for us to go to her house, mom said for some reason, Grandmamma Sharon was on her mind, like she felt that something was wrong. So, mom along with Jerome and myself caught the bus to check to make sure that everything was alright with her. When we got there, mom knocked on the door. "Oh... Oh... Oh... help me!" was a voice we heard coming from behind the door. "Mom, is that Grandma?" Jerome asked in a concern voice. "It sounds like her, let's check the door," responded Mom.

To our surprise, the door was unlocked. "Momma Sharon, are you okay?" mom called out. "No! I'm behind the door," Grandma replied in a very weak voice.

"My God, what happen?" asked mom as she tried helping her to her feet.

"No Ruth! No Ruth! I can't stand, it hurts too bad! Stop, Stop!" Grandma cried out. We have never seen our grandma in so much pain. As a matter of fact, we had never seen her in pain of any kind.

"What happened to you?" mom asked. "I missed a step and fell down the stairs," she replied, in a tearful voice. "Don't move. Let me call the ambulance.

Jackie, you and Jerome stay here with her while I make the call." said mom. It didn't take long for the ambulance arrived at the house.

"Don't worry Ms. Jones, we will take great care of you," the medical technician's comforting words were so soothing; that she calmed down and allowed them to put her on a stretcher and took her to the emergency room.

The parents of the children that we were allowed to play with, took us to the hospital in their car. Everyone sat in the waiting room while the doctor checked Grandma out. Mom was able to go in the room with her. "Jackie come sit here in the room with your grandmother while I call your dad to let him know what happened," Ruth said.

A few minutes later, mom was back, and the doctor walked in. "Well, well, what do we have here?" asked the doctor who was in charge. "I found her at the bottom of the stairs on the floor behind the door at her home. She told me she fell down the steps," mom expressed to the doctor.

"Miss Jones, what happened?" asked the doctor. *"Look here doctor, I don't want to be here and the only reason that I am, is because I am in pain and my daughter-in law insisted that I come. She already told you what happened, and I don't feel like saying it again."*

"Okay, let us take an x-ray of your leg and see what is going on," he replied. While Grandma went to get her leg x-rayed, the doctor looked at mom and asked, "Does she live with someone or by herself?"

"She's by herself," mom responded.

"It was good that you found her when you did. If you didn't, there's no telling what would have happened to her. But now she will need someone to help her for some weeks. She seems to be a feisty little lady, but she can't stay by herself, not right now."

"Well doctor, my mother-in law is very adamant about staying by herself. I will make sure that someone checks on her daily," mom told the doctor. At that time they rolled Grandma back in from having the x-ray of her leg done, she was in a lot of pain. We could tell by looking at her. As the doctor checked the x-rays out, he said, "Well, Miss Jones, your leg is broken, and we will have to put it in a cast."

Grandma didn't like that idea at all. The doctor told her that if he didn't put one on her leg it would not heal right. Finally, she agreed. After everything was done, we took a taxi back to Grandma's home. Two weeks passed and Grandma complained that the cast was slowing her down.

"If you don't take it off, I will!"

Mom tried talking her into allowing it to stay on for the entire eight weeks but all she said was "I'll think about it Ruth." With those words Mom knew that she needed to get in touch with her daughter that lives in Florida. After talking with Aunt Alice over the phone they were here in Savannah in one days. They stayed with Grandma for one week. After they returned home, someone checked on her daily. But a few weeks later, she did just what her heart sought after. She did just what she wanted to do. One day after work mom stopped by to check on her.

Well, just as mom thought, so it was. Grandma has taken a butcher knife and cut that cast off her leg. She refused to keep it on any longer. There wasn't anything anyone could have done or said to change her mind. Her leg healed but not like it should have. From that day she had problems with her leg. Everyone did what they could to help her out.

Today, mom looked more tired than usual; as she walked in the door her eyes looked so red, as if she hasn't slept in days. But she pushed that aside and headed for the kitchen because her family needed dinner. After sweating over that wooden stove, dinner was ready. The first thing, as she always did was fix dad's dinner first.

He was drinking and he looked at her and said, "What is this mess you fixed me? I don't want this!" With those words he got up off the bed and headed for the kitchen. As he walked, mom was trying to talk with him. "Well, Matt, what do you want to eat?" she asked in a very tired tone. "Not this mess!" He went straight to our back door; and threw the plate and the food outside into the plum trees. Not only that, he wasn't thinking about his children; he also took all the food that mom had worked so hard getting together, off the stove and threw it outside into the plum trees as well.

Now this was the first time since Mark died, we had seen our mom break down and cry. That night, mom didn't eat anything. She sent all of us to Grandmamma May and Uncle Pete's house, and they made sure we ate that night. When we returned home, Mom called us in and talked and prayed with us.

"Prayer is always helpful"

She said that she doesn't want us to have hate in our heart toward our dad, because God is all about love. But it was too late now; hate was there long before now.

Chapter 6

"Stand or fall in the mist"

That night at home, something happened. After throwing out our entire dinner, dad decided he wanted to go out with some of his friends. He was so upset that he walked out, forcefully closing the door behind him. About four hours later, there was a knock at the door. Mom went to open the door to see who was there.

Before she could get the door completely open, dad fell into her arms. "Matt, what happen to you?" Before he could say anything, he hit the floor. She tried so hard to hold him up, but he was just too heavy for her small body to handle. Blood was all over her. She tried to hide it, but you couldn't help but notice tears running down her face. I guess she thought he was going to die, well that's how he looked, lifeless.

"Be careful how you treat God's people?"

"Jackie, Jerome, help me, come help me with your father!" We stood there for a few seconds before we moved. "Come on! Help me get him on the bed," she shouted in a helpless tone. As we stood there for a very short time looking at each other thinking, why should we help him he didn't care about us earlier.

Besides we didn't want his blood on our clothes, but we did help and were very careful as we moved him. This was the very first time I had ever seen so much blood. Our Dad's eyes were swollen shut from the cuts and bruises. His body was messed up.

Blood was everywhere. I can recall Mom taking his blood soak clothes and putting them in the washtub filled with water. She was running back and forth, wrapping, and un-wrapping his wounds. She was throwing out washtubs of bloody water one after another.

Watching her working so hard to take care of him, we realize that this lady really loved this man. It seemed like she forgot how badly he treats her. Now look at him, who needs who now? He was in so much pain. Calling out to mom like she was God to take the pains away.

She could only do so much. But whenever dad cried out, she was right there. "What a woman," I thought to myself. The air in the house was full of the smell of old blood for days.

This man that we were looking at looked nothing like our father. I thought he was going to die. I couldn't understand why they didn't take him to the hospital to get the help he needed. But I guess Mom knew what was best. At this time, I began to feel bad, thinking it was my prayers that caused him to get in that car accident.

Or was this some sort of payback for how he treated mom over the years? God only knew, we must be very careful how we treat people, because one day we may need those people again to help us. Now I felt sorry for him. But a small part of me didn't, that hate that built up in me, covered up some of my compassion.

Hatred is a powerful weapon that won't let you love or forgive someone when they have victimized you in some way. Our ways are not God's way. He is a forgiven God, I was just too young to realize that.

But I still was wondering whether this accident would help him to change the way he treated his family, after he saw how Mom dedicated herself to taking care of him. One month passed and his condition started showing some improvements. While he was sick, Mom only worked on a Mondays and Thursdays of each week, for three to four hours on those days. She looked ten years older. That man was taking the life out of our mother and it didn't seem to bother her.

She was caring for him like she really loved him. Wow! A few more weeks passed, and mom decided it was time for her to return to work full time. Now that he was feeling better, you would think that he would have changed some of his ways. But did things change him? Yes, for about three months he was the father that we all wished for. He helped cook and he played with us. So, there was some good in him after all. But it didn't last long, heading into the fourth month he was back to his old self. Now Mom was back at work, working harder than before trying to play catch-up.

It looked as though she could barely put one foot in front of the other. She was so tired; you could see it all over her face. But did that stop her? No. She knew the only way for her family to eat was by her working. Our mom not only taught us, but she also showed us how to forgive and be a good person. There were times when mom would bring left over food home from her job, for us to have extra food to eat.

We, as children, hated that. Some of that food had a greenish color and smelled like it was freezer burn. Why would someone give something that they won't eat to others to eat? I couldn't understand that it didn't matter to me if mom cooked it or not. With all that, we were still blessed. There are so many people out there that didn't have that or anything to eat.

God has a way of keeping people on their knees. Dad had a very good job. He just didn't know how to budget his money, but I guess to him he did his best. He didn't have a man in his life to teach him how to be a good dad or a husband So, what can you expect?

Dad's boss knew that he was a hard worker. He just had a sickness that he couldn't control. He loved working with his hands. His boss owned a Cement Company, and he knew, by hiring dad, that the work would be done right, so he depended on him for a job well done.

Dad was the best concrete man in town. He helped with the construction of so many buildings here in downtown Savannah. Because dad was a great worker, and his boss knew his problems, so he helped Mom out as   much as he and his wife could.

During the Christmas holidays, he would bring us fruits and toys. On thanksgiving he gave us a turkey, some sweet potatoes, fruits, and other goodies. He was a good man; he wanted to make sure that our holidays were the greatest. For children, Christmas should be the best time of the year.

"Oh boy Christmas dinner"

For our family, it was a very joyful time. Not only did dad's boss make their holiday's special, but the family members did as well. Coming together to share a meal, but the best gift that the family had, that didn't cost them any money, was the gift of laughter.

That time together seemed to roll by fast, but it was fun while it lasted. Now it was three weeks into the New Year, and we noticed Mom sitting in a chair looking as if she was thinking about something very hard. She looked so sad. "Mom, is something wrong?" asked Jerome.

"It's okay baby, but I do need to talk with Jackie," she responded.

"What about me?" Jerome asked.

"Not at this time, son, maybe later."

"Jack...i.e ! Jerome yelled.

"Boy, what do you want? And why are you yelling out my name like that?"

"Girl, momma wants you."

"Okay, I'm coming," I responded to him. As I walked in, I recognized an old familiar look on Mom's face. "Yes, mama you wanted me?"

"Yes, have a seat I need to talk with you about something," she said. As I sat down, I began to wonder what was wrong now. That look on her face reminded me of a time when Mom called all of us in before.

Tim was about three months old, when she told us that she was going away for a while, and that we were going to stay with Grandma May, Uncle Pete, and his wife until she got back. I recalled her leaving and we cried on and off for weeks. We thought that we were so bad that she just had to get away from us. It appears that she was gone for years. But they were only gone for about six months. So, I braced myself for what was about to come. "Mom, are you about to leave us again?" I asked, after thinking for a while.

"No Jackie, why would you ask me that question?"

"Because you have that same look that you had when you left us before," I replied in a sad voice.

"I am sitting here thinking about why you are acting up so, and what about all these fights you are getting in?"

"Who? Me? Mom, I only fight when someone starts one with me first," I answered. "I was told that you started a fight with our neighbor's daughter on the way home from school today. Is that true?" she asked.

"No-ma'am, I didn't start it; she did, but there was a fight," I replied. "Why, what happen?"

"It was a left-over fight that happen last weekend when all the adults when grocery shopping." "Jackie, who was fighting last week?" she asked.

"All of us, our family was against their family, because of those pear trees in the field." "Where were the older children?" she asked. "They were fighting the older ones on their side." "What?" she said in disbelieve. "What does the pear trees have to do with a fight?" "Mom, for the last twoweeks we wanted some pears off that tree in the field behind our house. Each time we go and pick some of them, someone would shoot at us. When we found out who it was, they wanted to fight us."

"Was Step there, if so, why she didn't stop it?" Mom asked. "Step was there, but she was fighting too."

"I don't like that. We didn't teach you all to fight, especially not your neighbor. I need to talk with all of you later. This is not over yet. I will get back with you all later," Mom said.

"Okay mom." As I walked away, Mom called my name. "Jackie, but... well,who won the fight?"

I was surprised by that question. "Oh, Mom, of course we did every time! She thought that I didn't see that small smile on her face, BUT I DID."

Mom did talk with us concerning the fighting.   But the next year the same thing happened again. We would fight one another makeup and be friends and do it all repeatedly. They finally told us that it was only blanks in that gun. They just like scaring us; it worked the first and second time, but not the third time.

CHAPTER 7

"Running in the sun"

This day started out great. Our parents were all gone to work, and we were at our Grandma May's house. We all love playing with each other, but for some reason my cousin Mary and I were having a difference of opinion. It looked like we weren't going to agree on anything that morning. Sometimes we as children get upset with each other over some of the craziest things; then later forget what it was all about.

Mary said something, then I said something; before we both realized it, we were striking one another. "Grandmamma, Mary and Jackie are fighting one another!" yelled one of our cousins. "What! I know they are not!" she said. We stopped when we heard Grandmamma's voice.

I started running toward the house, but Mary was so upset with me she picked up a piece of broken glass that was near her I didn't know she had it until I turned around to see whether she was running after me. But when I turned around, that broken glass caught the side of my face. My cousin Mary had a great left-handed throw.

"You can't catch me"

I cried out in pain as blood ran down my face. I was screaming, and I thought I was going to die. "Jackie, what is wrong with you?" Grandma May asked. I couldn't say a word from screaming so loud. Mary was standing there crying as well; "I'm sorry... I'm sorry.

"I am so sorry, Jackie"

I didn't mean to do it!" Mary said over and over. "Oh my god, come here Jackie! I will deal with you later, Mary. Go inside the house and sit down until I am done with Jackie!" said Grandma May.

With her gentle care, she washed my face and packed the wound with some spider webs and covered it with a large Band-Aid. After she was done with me, I sat in a chair for about ten minutes. "Come here Mary and Jackie." Grandma sat in her chair and talked with us. She was so upset with the both of us; she told us how family supports each other.

Regardless of what happened, we should never hurt another member of our family; God love families and shall never hurt what God loves. We knew that fighting with family was wrong. When she was done talking with us for thirty minutes, we thought it was over.

But then she said something that really messed me up. "Jackie, you and Mary go outside and bring me a switch."

"But grandma not me. Look what she did to me!" I spoke. I was still upset because of my face and for me to get a whipping; I thought that was unfair to me.

"I see your face; now move it. Do as you are told!" she replied. We both walked outside, moving slow, we were looking for one that with one hit it would break. "What is taking so long? Do I need to get it myself?" Grandma yelled. After carefully collecting the perfect one, we walked in and gave it to her. But then she told us to stand there and not to move. One hit and it did just what we wanted; it broke in half.

"Okay. I see y'all want to play games. I will get it myself." As she walked out the door, we looked at one another and broke out crying. It didn't do any good; she came in and sat in her chair. She told us we had better stand there because she wasn't going to get up out of her chair.

She had a long skinny switch that made a sound as she whipped both of us. From that day on my cousin and I never fought one another again. About three months later, we were all sitting outside talking, when Mom somehow talked Uncle Pete into letting her drive his car. At first, he didn't want to let her drive.

But he finally decided to let her try it; wow, what was he thinking? A big smile came to her face, like a child that just got everything they wanted for Christmas. And that was a rare thing to see, a big smile on

Mom's face. "Okay, Pete, what do I do now?" she asked her brother with excitement.

"What Ruth? I assumed that you knew how to start a car," he said. "Move over. Let me show you. I'll start it, then I will turn it off and you will do it. So, watch and see what I do."

"Okay now you do it." Mom tried it and it worked. But that wasn't the problem what came when she put it in the drive. Before we knew what happened, Mom made an extra row in Grandma's corn field. "Pete, Pete, it's getting away from me! What do I do now Pete?" she asked as she cut through the corn field.

"Hit the brake, Ruth! Hit the brake now!"

"Okay, what's that?" she replied. Uncle Pete reached over and hit the brake and turned off the car.

"Here take your keys, that's aright, I don't want to learn, I'm sorry about your car!" mom repeated. But Pete was okay his car wasn't damaged due to what happened. Mom decided not to ever ask anyone about teaching her how to drive a car again. We all stood around after seeing what happened and we all started laughing. Uncle Pete did as well.

There were times of great joy and laughter in our family. Isn't that what God want for us? That is to be happy. It made us very happy to see our uncles come together for cookouts, the livestock in our family was just like a meal on the table, umm... good. Uncle John, Uncle Robert and Uncle Pete seemed to have so much excitement whenever the Fourth of July was approaching. They were like kids again. They would pick out one of the best hogs to barbeque.

Following the clean-out period, they killed it and tied it to a branch of a big tree. Then they would slice it down the middle, with a big tub under it to catch all the hog organs. All the equipment was set in place and a smell would fill the air and the minds for a very long time.

But there would be something extra that would make this day different from all the other Fourth of July cookouts. On this day, everyone in the neighborhood was family. Family members came home from up North and all around. The cookout is on now. The excitement was in the air.

"BarBQ time"

Not only was the smell in the air but on us as well. My cousin Paige her Mom Aunt Cathy, and all her siblings were here from up North. Not only were we cousins but best of friends. We have always enjoyed each other. Climbing trees, playing house with other family members was fun for us. The smell of freshly cut green grass and the smell of that barbeque - wow!

The tables were set so beautifully with cakes, hot dogs, watermelons and so many other goodies. Everyone sitting or standing around, children playing and others busy doing their thing. But now the family was about to get that extra helping of fun and laugher. Our cousin, Jason, needed to use the outhouse, but there was something else using it as well. As he sat there, to his surprise he noticed that he wasn't alone.

As everyone was doing their own thing, there was a loud noise coming from the outhouse direction. "Help me..., Daddy! Help me!" His dad heard his son screaming out for help. Uncle Robert stopped what he was doing, running to see what was going on. "Help, help me.... I don't want to die....

Daddy it's going to eat me!" He screamed as he ran as fast as his legs could carry him. But there was something close behind him coming up fast. Everyone stopped to see what was going on.

Everyone was yelling "come on! You better run faster than that run, run." Uncle Pete ran in his house to get his gun. He gave the gun to Uncle Robert; he aimed it ready to fire. "Run son, run! Come on!" Uncle Robert yelled. Jason ran toward the house his pants was around his knees which caused him not to run as fast as he usually did. As Jason approached the house, Uncle Robert stood waiting for the kill.

No-one was sure of what it was, but it was big and grew larger as it grew closer. "I see it!" Uncle Pete yelled, "oh my God it's a big alligator!" Uncle Robert

"Please don't eat me!"

fired once. Boom! Then he fired again. Boom! He hit that alligator head on. "You got him, you got him!" Uncle Pete said.

What a day to remember. After the kill, all the men took it and hung it up in that big Chinaberry tree in the front yard. A news reporter from the newspaper came out. They took pictures of Uncle Robert in front of that gator. It was a big write up in the newspaper. It was the talk of the town for many years.

CHAPTER 8

"The plans were already set"

Coming together with the family for cookouts was always great. And there were so many other beautiful times to remember. One good thing. about our uncles and aunts, they never thought that they were too grown up to play with us. Saturday evenings during the summer months were baseballgame time. The adults were against the young people. It was fun, although we didn't win all the time, but there were times when we did win. People in the neighborhood came out just to watch us play.

Some of the older people would be on the sideline. "Come on kids, you can win. Yes you can, you are stronger and faster than they are. Come on, hit that ball!" they all yelled. This was such a joy to hear them rooting for us like that. Oh yes, love was all around us. Other people saw it and were very jealous of it. It was always some kind of excitement in our family. We loved one another. If there were issues with the adults, us children didn't know about it. The adults allowed us to be children.

Even during the time of sadness, the family was strong as they stood together. One day comes to mind. This morning we all went to school as usual. Things were going great. Aunt Betty came by the school that evening after school for a meeting. As we sat there in the library reading some books, waiting until her meeting was over, the school secretary walked in with a note that she needed to call home. She told us to stay until she called home.

Within three minutes, she was back saying that we needed to leave now. It seemed like she couldn't get home fast enough. We walked in the door and Grandma May pulled her to the side to talk with her. Aunt Betty walked into her bedroom and just stayed there.

When she came out, she looked so sad. There was a dark cloud hanging over the house that had brought so much joy to our lives.

We didn't understand what was happening at that time, but I felt the sadness in the house. "What's wrong with Aunt Betty?" Step asked Grandma May.

"Their baby· girl, Kim, is very sick," Grandma replied.

"What is wrong with Kim?" I asked.

"We don't know. Your Uncle Pete called the ambulance, but they haven't shown up yet."

Just as Grandma was speaking, I heard an old cry that I recognized. "No Kim, don't leave me! Wake up! Pete!" Aunt Betty screamed out. Uncle Pete ran in their room. "Please wake up baby!" Aunt Betty cried out with a broken heart. The ambulance and police came at that time. But it was too late. Baby Kim had already taken her flight out in the arms of an angel sent by God. They checked her over; the police asked some questions for their report.

Afterwards, they took Baby Kim to the hospital. Aunt Betty cried for many, many months. Uncle Pete tried comforting her. He was hurting, but he didn't want her to see his pain, but it was there. After the home-going service, Aunt Betty looked so sad. The laughter and joy for a while was gone. But the family banded together with prayer and love.

Things slowly returned to somewhat normal for some people. But it took a while for Aunt Betty to come around. About a year passed and she was sitting at the table reading her bible. She spoke for the first time about Kim. We sat there listening to what she said.

"A mother's heart"

"My sweet baby looked so beautiful. As she laid there, her eyes were fixed toward the corner of the room. She was smiling as if there were angels in the room with us. Each time I called her name, she turned her head and looked at me as to say with her eyes, mama I am alright. I am going home with the lord. I am happy, don't cry. And with a very small smile, *Kim* turned back toward the wall."

"She looked at that same spot for ten minutes, and then she closed her tiny eyes for the last time," Aunt Betty said.

A Tender Rose

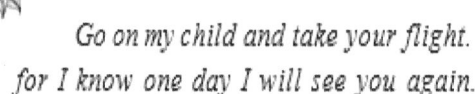

Go on my child and take your flight.
for I know one day I will see you again.

God noticed a tender young beautiful rose

in his garden of youth and picked it; oh yes

we will miss you.

But I know that God will mend my broken heart

In due time, your time here was very short.

But the Lord will give me hope and strength to

Carry on until one day when He calls me home.

Just to hear her talk about it was hurtful. The tears were rolling down her face as she talked about Kim. But it seemed to help her by talking; because from that day, she was able get up and do some things that she hadn't done for months.

"It hurts but I need to talk"

Yes, they had other children and they loved them as well. But one has nothing to do with the other, each of them had they own place in their hearts.

Things we learned as children was that God is in control of everything in our lives. Even when there is sadness, pain or laughter, God loves us. Looking at my family of such strong faith in God made things better. Here is another Sunday and we are in church as usual. This Sunday we have a one-of-a-kind speaker. Someone people don't talk about much or give her any credit for anything. But as she always said God has her record.

And if he knows, don't worry about what people say or don't say. We must do to please God, not man. On this Sunday, Grandma May preached the word. She had a rhythmical walk as she sang her favorite song. "Walk with me, Lord, Lord, walk with me." She stood there on the floor in front of a table with her shawl thrown around her shoulder.

When she opened her mouth to speak, the words of the Lord she spoke were so very powerful. She taught us so many wonderful things. What she was at church was the same as at home. At home during the day when the twelve o'clock whistle blew, we knew what time it was. Lunchtime!

Grandma May would read a scripture and prayed with us. No prayer, no lunch. Those were the rules, no exception. We learned that going to church wasn't so bad. Our comfort place was at Grandma May's house. Every opportunity we had, our surrounding cousins and friends would come together under a big walnut tree that was in Grandma's backyard.

It was fun playing under that big tree. We fixed up a playhouse and we'd play at cooking. Making mud cakes, using grass for our collard greens, and pulled grass by the roots for our baby dolls. There were always some excitements in some sort of way.

But the best game we played was church, mimicking the preachers and the saints on how they act. This was our usual thing we did almost every day. If we weren't climbing trees or playing house, we were playing church. As we sang songs and pretended like we were praising the Lord; we were having fun until I looked up toward the heavens, why, I don't know.

My eyes were closed; when I opened them, there was something waiting to fall on me. A big nest of caterpillars fell on my back. "AH ! AH!

"Get them off of me!"

They're all over me!" Screaming and tearing my shirt off as I ran. Aunt Betty ran to see what was going on. "Jackie, what is wrong?" "They are all over me!" Pulling on my shirt, shaking as though I was about to have a nervous breakdown. "They are all over me!" I responded in a tearful voice.

"Come here. Let me check, calm down Jackie." She checked me out to make sure that there wasn't any more on me. They were all off, but I was so upset I couldn't stop trembling with fear.

"They are gone baby, see look," she said in a sympathetic voice. "Come on Jackie, let's go in the house." As we walked, tears were still falling. "Don't cry. Sit here. I'll get you something to drink, and when you feel better, you may go back outside to play." I sat there for one hour before I decided to go back outside.

From that day on, I was afraid of any type of worms. It took me a while before going back to play under that walnut tree. But there was always something to get into. Staying busy and having fun was great, no pain when there was laughter.

We weren't always good; there were times when Uncle Pete had to whip us. His whipping we didn't mind. He was so loving in what he did. He would send us in the bedroom to wait on him. As we sat there wondering what was going to happen; there he comes in with a smile on his face and says; "Listen, when I hit the bed, you all cry like I'm hitting you. Okay?" "YES SIR!" we all answered. We would put on a good show for the other adults. Then he would say something like this: "If you all do it again it will be worse the next time, do ya'll understand? Our reply would be "YES SIR!" Before walking out the room we would wet our eyes with water to look as if we were crying. He just didn't like whipping us and we loved it.

Things were great for now. Now that winter was here, the weather seemed to be so cold that your breath appeared to freeze in the air.

Walking outside to get wood for the stove was a difficult task. The ground was frozen hard, and ice hung from the house. Everyone had to be very careful walking or looking up whenever you went outside. If we made the wrong step, we could lose our footing and fall, and could severely damage our body, or look up and a piece of ice may fall off and hit you in your eye. But during everything, there were a lot of good times.

Dad showed us how to use a long saw to have wood for the stove, one person at each end. Pushing back and forth sawed the wood into smaller pieces. There were some good times with Dad, which made Mom very happy. After cutting the wood, we would sit around the stove talking, playing games, and singing songs. The fire in that stove felt so good.

Chapter 9

"The jokester"

On this cold winter night everything felt so good. A since of peace was in the house. Happiness was in the atmosphere. Red seems draw our little brother's attention. "Wow, that stove is the color of red!" Tim said. "Yes, and it would cook you alive too," Step said, laughing out loud. Tim didn't think that he was that close to the stove. Until Mom said, "Tim, you are playing too close to the stove baby."

"Okay Mom. I will be careful," he said.

"Tim! What did I say? You need to move. You are too close to that sto...!" Before Mom could complete her sentence, Tim had backed up not noticing where he was, and his bottom touched that red-hot stove. Tim screamed out a cry that seemed so painful that pierced your very soul and sent chills though your body. "Ouch…! Ouch...! Ouch...! I'm on fire! Ouch! Mama help me!

"Fire has a tattoo of its own"

Mama its hurts so bad!" he said. Tim was screaming as loud as he could.I felt so sorry for him, just by looking at him, you could imagine his pain. I didn't think the boy could scream so loud. It was so loud I believed everyone on our street could hear him. The stove was so hot it was red like fire. The smell reminded me of when Grandma's leg was burned by the hot grease.

Tim's bottom looked like someone had branded him with a hot poker iron. My baby brother was in so much pain, he cried for hours, so it seemed. Mom knew exactly what to do. With that tender hand of loving care and nurturing, he was feeling better just from the sound of her sweet voice.

She got Uncle Pete to take him to the emergency room for treatment. Tim suffered with third-degree burns. He couldn't sit for weeks because of the burn being too sensitive to touch. He was in pain for weeks. Step was there taking good care of him while Mom was at work; after about three weeks, he was feeling better.

After that incident, Mom didn't have to tell Tim to stay away from the stove anymore. We still had one or two nights a week fun time when Dad wasn't drinking. He taught us some new songs and word games. One word play I can recall was with the word (preface), and it goes like this, PETER RABBIT EAT FISH, ALLIGATOR CATCH EVE, EVE CATCH ALLIGATOR, FISH EAT RAW POTATOES. There were so many other fun things that he taught us.

There were times when Dad seemed like a real family man.And when that happened, the whole atmosphere at home changed. But for some reason, there was an old lady who lived on the side of us who didn't think he was a good man at all. There were days when she would stand in her yard calling out to mom. "Ruth, put that evil man out. He is no-good, and you can do better than that!"

That always scared us. She couldn't stand Dad, or maybe she saw him for what he really was inside. That couldn't have been the case. She didn't like children neither. Each day we had to pass her house to get to Grandma May's house. There was no other way around it. If she saw us about to pass her house, she would run outside with a hoe, chasing behind us.

"You kids leave from in front of my house, now!" she would yell. We would run as fast as we could. For us to get the water, we had to pass the old lady's house. Because the water pump was in Grandma's yard. There were so many times we had to cross to the other side of the street to get by.

There was a ditch in front of that same lady's house, which had some nice size crawfishes. After Bill showed us how to catch and cook them; it was hard to stay away from that ditch. So, any time we had an opportunity to catch some, we did. About two weeks passed and we didn't see her. We began to wonder where she was.

Mom knew the lady's family, and she asked questions concerning her were abouts. We found out from Mom that the old lady had taken sick, and her family moved her away. We didn't want anything bad to happen to her, but now it was much better going back and forth to Grandma's house with no problems. But now that the old lady had moved out, another family moved in. In this family, was a girl my age. Her name was Beverly.

I could see a whole new way of life was opening to me through Beverly; she became my best friend. One day as were talking and playing, Beverly came up with an idea. "Jackie, why don't you and I become blood sisters?"

"Blood sisters, what'sthat? I never heard of that before," I said.

"What! You never heard of that before?" she asked. "Let me show you. Wait here. I'll be back." Beverly ran inside her house and when she returned, she had a safety pin in her hand.

"What are you going to do with that pin, Beverly?" I asked.

"Calm down, it's not that bad. This is how it works; I'm going to stick myself until my finger bleeds. Then I will do the same thing to your finger. Afterwards, we would put our fingers together and mixed our blood. See, like this. Now, we are blood sisters," she explained. "Okay, that didn't hurt," I responded.

"Look we are sisters now!"

It was so good to have someone else my age to play with. Beverly introduced me to other members of her family. Her family was very nice. She had a big family, ten brothers and seven sisters, wow! She had a brother by the name of Chris; He told Beverly that he liked me, and I was a very pretty girl. "Beverly, I like him too. Tell him that for me, okay?"

"Okay I will," said Beverly.

This was different. A boy liked me. I said to myself. Well, he looked ok. As kids, adults called this puppy love. Well, it didn't seem like puppy love to me. We both were teenagers. What is love at our age? One day, we were all outside talking and playing around.

He decided that he wanted to kiss me. But at that time, I told him NO! But things were changing between us. He would always find something nice to say to me, buy me candy and send notes by Beverly to give me. As I read each note and ate the candy, I thought to myself, WOW, here's someone that thinks I am beautiful. Me! Right, another joke. Who and why would he think that? No one else does.

As I sat there on the steps of our back door thinking to myself. "The next time he wants to kiss me, I will let him.

"Jackie! What are you doing? Can you come over?" Beverly yelled.

"I guess. What's going on?" Our houses were next door. All I had to do was walk out my yard and in her.

As we sat there on her porch talking and laughing, Chris walked up. "Hey Jackie, how are you?" he said as he walked into his house. All I could do was smile.

Beverly looked at me and told me how much he liked me. One day, Jerome caught us kissing. "Jackie, what are you doing? I'm going to tell Mama!"

"Tell her what?" I asked.

"You and that boy were kissing," he said.

"And, so what, tell I don't care," I responded, thinking that just because I said it that way, Jerome wouldn't say anything.

But Mr. Big Mouth did. That afternoon, Mom came home from a hard day of work, and Jerome couldn't wait to open his big mouth. But Mom was so tried, that he decided not to say anything to her. "You owe me," he said.

"Owe you what?" Chris liked me and I liked him and that's all that mattered to me.

Things were going well, so I thought, for this teenager puppy love thing. But then one day, I saw Chris with another girl. If this was puppy love, so they say, why does it hurt so badly? "Why would he do this to me?" I asked myself.

His sister and I remained friends. Beverly also had an older brother who just fell head over heels for my sister Step, and she for him. They dated for a long time. Chris and the whole family were best of friends. As time passed, I got over it.

CHAPTER 10

"Set it off"

Today is a beautiful spring day with the birds singing and the sun shining so bright. Jerome and I were sitting on the porch looking at all our wish cars go by. Wish cars are the cars we said we will buy when we grow up. But also, on this day, we will see another side of life.

We were introduced to some other members of Dad's family. The only person we knew was Grandma Sharon, and we loved her dearly. We didn't know much about his other family members. Occasionally, he would talk about them. So, this would be our second time meeting of them.

There were two uncles that lived here, one by the name of Uncle Charles Jones and the other was Uncle Michael Jones. Uncle Michael was a preacher. And Uncle Charles was a composer, played instruments, and was a singer; he had his own band. He gave us some money the first time he met us and every time after that. Now that was a good uncle.

Dad also had sisters, Aunt Alice and her husband Uncle Willie, and Aunt Rose, who live up north, and there was another aunt that I barely remember, but what I remember about her was she was a tall slim, fair-skinned beautiful lady and she always gave us a big glass of home-made lemonade in a glass with yellow flowers painted on them. She died when we were still very young.

Getting to know Aunt Alice and Uncle Willie whenever they came to town for a visit was a good thing, but it also was scary sometimes.

Aunt Alice didn't play, not at all. She had so many similar ways, just like her mother, Grandma Sharon.

She would treat you right if you didn't cross her in the wrong way. They would always bring us something. They showed us that they loved and cared about us in many ways. We always looked forward to their visit.

At one point they wanted to take us home to live with them. But Dad said NO WAY! If we starve, we will all starve together". He didn't believe in splitting up his family.

On this 10th day of August, we would see another side of our Aunt Alice that we had never seen before. I remember Step, Jerome, Tim, and I were all at the house and suddenly there was a loud noise. We couldn't believe our eyes. Our dad and his sister were arguing.

Now, that wasn't unusual but there was also another person involved. She was their cousin Cindy. We didn't know what was going on between them, Dad and Cindy were fighting like cats and dogs. We had never seen that before. This didn't happen on moms' side of the family, well not among the adults. Yes, we as children would fight other people that is our ages, but not family members; especially after that whipping Grandma gave Mary and myself for fighting each other. But here all three of them were really going at it badly.

I turned around and their cousin Cindy was lying outside on our front porch. She was covered in blood. What happened to her?" Tim asked. "I don't know," answered Step. Later we found out that Dad had picked her up and thrown her through our front window.

Why would a man do that to a woman? And she is so tiny. It hurt me to my heart to see her lying on the porch like that. But why should I wonder why? The way he used to hit our mom this should not be surprising to me.

As we looked on, Aunt Alice was so upset; "Matt, why did you do that? That was not called for; she is family and a lady, now I will show you what this lady can do!" Aunt Alice was so outraged she turned around and headed straight for her car; we had no idea why.

But as she walked, she went for the trunk of her car. She opened it and browsed around in it for about fifteen seconds and then closed it. We noticed that she had something in her hand. But what was it?

A gun! We all ran for cover because if she started shooting, a bullet has no eyes to see where it is going. Aunt Alice walked up to dad, and, without fear, she put that gun up to his head and said, "You are mouthing off so much. I'm not Ruth, now say another word and I will blow your head off!" she said to him in a very angry tone. The fear that came over his face was indescribable.

"Do you want to try me, now?"

He knew his sister wasn't playing. Aunt Alice stood there. "Alice, calm down. Put the gun down, baby," said Uncle Willie. "No, Matt didn't have to throw Cindy though that window. She is family, and families don'tdo that!"

"Come on, give me the gun, give it to me." Uncle Willie's words were soothing to her.

"Not until Matt apologizes to Cindy," she said.

"Okay, Alice, I just get to upset; and Cindy said something to me and ticked me off. Before I knew what happened I had picked her up and thrown her."

"I am so sorry!" he said to Alice.

"What? Don't tell me tell Cindy!"

Dad turned around and walked outside; Cindy was sitting on the porch, lying up against the house covered with cuts and blood. "Cindy. I'm so sorry about what I did to you. I'll help you up.

Please forgive me, I was so angry at what you said. I don't know what came over me, come on," he said. Poor Cindy was in a lot of pain. She didn't say a word. All she did was moan in pain.

Aunt Alice followed Dad around with that gun up to his head; until he apologized. After he did, she removed the gun and things calmed down. We were happy to see this. We loved our Aunt Alice; she was one of a kind; there aren't too many in this world like her. We are happy about that because she is authentic.

During all of this, Mom was on the sideline praying. She knows firsthand what can happen when you try to stop an angry person when they are fighting. Things can turn and you yourself can get killed. Whenever people are drinking anything can happen, and the word sorry will not bring back life.

Cindy looked like she was in so much pain; nothing shall have caused a man to do any woman like that. Blood was everywhere. "Step; go inside and see if you can find a dress for her to put on, please baby. Mom said. I felt so sorry for cousin Cindy. Okay mom I believe I may have some in Jackie's room she may be able to wear."

While Step was looking for a dress, Mom and Aunt Alice helped Cindy by washing and nursing her wounds. Step found a very nice greenish dress for her to put on. I wondered; would I be like Aunt Alice when I grow up? I thought to myself.

Sure, there were times in my life when I rebelled against my parents and the adults in the family. I was a fighter too; for many years I didn't back down for anyone. I didn't care whether they were older than me. My aunt showed me how to stand up for myself and not to back down for any reason.

Dad always said if we ever had to fight, we better win; because if we didn't, he would whip us himself when we got home. So, I won every time. Mom didn't like the idea that I was fighting.

Somebody had to do it. I didn't give Jerome an opportunity to fight; when someone approached him to start one, I was there. Maybe he knew how; but I never found out. Yes, I have a very strong will to survive. Our mom is a prime display of strength.

She was a very hard worker. Later, we found out what type of work she did. She worked as a maid raising other people's children, cleaning, and cooking for them. But it put food on our table and clothes on our backs, which was the only reason she did it. She didn't like it, but she did what she had to do. Whatever dresses and skirts that weren't given to us or what she wasn't able to buy she made them by hand.

It was heartbreaking seeing her walk that long road; hot during the summer and cold during the winter months; coming home carrying heavy bags, sometimes. I believe every step was a step of love for her family.

One Saturday, we were playing in the yard and a nice car drove up. Mom walked to the car to talk with the man that was driving. To our surprise, it was her boss. He had stopped by to pick us up; he said that he wanted to take us to see his horse farm. Mom went with us; it was so much fun.

They had cows, hogs, and ponies, well, we weren't thrilled over the hogs because we see them every day. We rode on the horses a few times. It was scary but fun.

"Look at the horse"

Afterward, they took us to their house for some cake and ice cream. It tasted so good. Just before we left, we met their daughter. She was in the bed, her body looked deformed. I looked at her from a distance. I was afraid to get too close to her for I never have seen anyone like that before.

After we visited their home, they took us home. As we walked in our door, I looked at Mom and asked, "what was wrong with that lady in the bed?"

"Well Jackie, she has something called polio. It affected her spinal cord, that is why her body is twisted the way it is." Mom added, "It's hard for me sometimes because I have to lift her up in order to wash and dress her." "Now, I see why your back gives you so many problems," I replied.

We learned a very important lesson that weekend. Things in life don't always come easy; you must sacrifice a lot for the people you love, even if it hurts you.

Chapter 11

"Life surprises"

But with all the fun, the pain in my life was always hidden behind my smile. As time passed, I grew up and saw things in a different light. Grandma May always have something for us to do. She kept us busy. Working in the family vegetable garden and helping where we were needed, was good training for all of us.

Grandma May has an in-home ironing job, where she would take in ironing for pay. She showed me how to iron shirts and pants. I was so proud of my accomplishment. I felt especially proud when grandma gave me some money for doing such a great job. This was great because now I had my own money to go to the store.

She was so happy with my work that she also showed me how to scrub the kitchen wooden floor with bleach and soap powder until it looked yellow. That was an extra fifty cents. I also earned extra money by babysitting my cousins. We also had to help clean our great aunt's house. We called her *Big Mama*- she was Grandma May's sister. She couldn't do very much because she had crippling arthritis.

It was also a joy combing her long beautiful hair that went down her back. We were told that she and Grandma May were from the Navaho tribe, and she looked like it too. We didn't think that she had any children because she raised one of my brothers. Later, we found out that she had three children; but they had all moved away except her son, who was married. He was so funny; he was always trying to scare us.

There were nights when we were in our room getting ready for bed, and we would hear sounds of scary scratching and meowing coming from the outside of our room window. We all jumped up, running and screaming, "Mom, something is at our window!" yelled Jerome.

Mom knew who it was. "Shorty, is that you? ·" she asked. "Yah it's me, Ruth," he replied. "Come on in and stop scaring my children," I remember that he was a very short man; maybe that is why they called him *Shorty*.

We loved him coming around. He was fun to be around as well. But I do remember one night we were sitting around the dinner table and there was a knock at the door. Mom answered it. Whoever that is, told Mom something that caused her to cry out. She began crying and we wanted to know why our mother was crying. All we could hear was her saying, "Oh no! Oh no, not Shorty. Lord, not Shorty!"

"Mama please "don't cry"

She cried for a while; later she told us that a man shot and killed Shorty. That was a very sad night. We didn't understand why anyone would want to kill him.

We missed him coming around. For weeks, we were listening to the sound at the window, but all we heard was silence. Big Mama grieved for a long time because of the loss of her one and only son. It was a while before Big Mama was able to communicate with the family. When she did, it was always a joy listening to what she had to say. We were pleased to see that she was feeling better.

Big Mama had plum trees and the plums tasted so good. They were big and purple and were the juiciest. So, when it was plum season, we knew just where to go. We had fruit trees and berry bushes all around us. If we didn't get the pears, we had plums. If not plums, we had hock-a-berries, and we had all kinds of goodies. If we couldn't get it one way, we got them another way.

There was always a fruit man coming by, selling watermelons. Not only did he sell watermelon, but other fruits and vegetables as well. Once a week, he would just bring extra loads to give to the livestock.

As we were growing and playing, I was changing all the time. My baby sister was my shadow. She followed me around always, but that was fine; I liked looking out for her. Tim was always getting into something as well, but he was the joy of our life. It was good to have someone looking up to me for help.

"Jackie, come on, you promised me that you will play jacks with me," Katrina said. With Katrina, one game of any kind was never enough. "Katrina, go ask Jerome," I answered. "No, Jackie! All Jerome wants to do is read and play those dumb word puzzle games!"

I can't say too much about that because it was true. As Jerome was getting older, there were many times when all he wanted to do was listen to old gospel music, and play those word puzzle games. He was an old bookworm to me.

He was a strange-acting young man sometimes. But it didn't stop me from trying new things. After seeing what Mom went through with her job, I decided to help sometimes by cooking for her. I liked coming up with weird things to cook. I liked cooking, but the best part of the whole thing was getting Tim, Katrina, and Jerome to taste whatever I cooked.

There was a big mulberry tree in our backyard. When the season comes, we would pick the fruit and eat until we were full, and just couldn't eat anymore.

"Jerome, what do you think about me trying mulberry dumplings?" I asked. "What?" he responded. "Well, I never cooked mulberries before; I wonder how they would taste."

During this time, Mom was at work so I decided to try to make some Mulberry dumplings, like when Mom made her remarkable Blackberry dumplings. Everything was set, and all was going well: the sugar and all the ingredients were inside the pot. *'Oh, it smells so good!'* I was thinking to myself.

I walked away to wash an old pot I had used, and when I returned to check on the pot, to my big surprise there weren't only mulberries in that pot; it was filled with green worms! I dropped the pot top and screamed so loud that Jerome came running.

"Girl, what is wrong with you?" he asked.

"Look! Look in the pot! Look!" I was yelling.

Jerome walked over and looked. "Girl, worms in that pot? Who's going to eat that? Not me!" he said as he walked away laughing. I remembered that Bill had once told us that those berries were filled with worms when we were eating them off the tree. But no, we didn't believe him, because they tasted so good. I wanted to surprise Mom with the new dessert when she comes home.

But now she was going to be upset because I used up all her sugar trying to get that pot to taste good. I learned my lesson that sometimes I needed to listen to my elders. What an expensive way to learn that he was telling us the truth, after all. After that day, we didn't eat any more of those berries, we had enough worms inside us to last us a lifetime now.

That next morning was Saturday, which was our wash day. I opened my dresser drawer to get something to wear. As I opened it and picked up a shirt, something moved. I yelled out, "Mom, help! Something is in my drawer! Come here! What is this?"

Mom rushed in to see what was wrong. As she walked in, I was on top of my bed jumping up and down, screaming at the top of my voice.

"Calm down Jackie, let me see what is in the drawer," she said. Mom walked over and opened the drawer. I heard a strange sound. "Oh Jackie, it's only a few baby mice," she told me.

I walked over to look.

"Mom, they have no hair; they are so ugly, and they smell too!"

"Yes, I know. I will get rid of them this morning. You won't have to worry about this anymore," she said.

Mom did just as she said. We don't know what she did, but we never had that problem anymore.

Not only was our family the foundation of our growth, but there were also adults in our neighborhood who took part in the upbringing of the children. There was one lady by the name of Mrs. Maria. Mrs. Maria was another church-going lady but from a different background. Every summer during our school break, she would ensure we attended summer Bible school. Learning songs and God was so much fun. Just thinking about those cookies and juice reminds me of a taste that I haven't tasted since then.

This was on top of what the family did. She just made going to church so much fun and we couldn't wait until the next time.

And then there was another lady and her husband, Mr. and Mrs. Jackson- that loved us all children as well. They had such a heart for kids that they donated a portion of their property to the community to build a playground so that we could all have a place to play. They threw parties to raise money for play equipment. Mrs. Jackson didn't stop there; she wanted to make sure that we had something to eat during the summer months too, so she applied for free lunches to be delivered at the park, just like all the other surrounding parks.

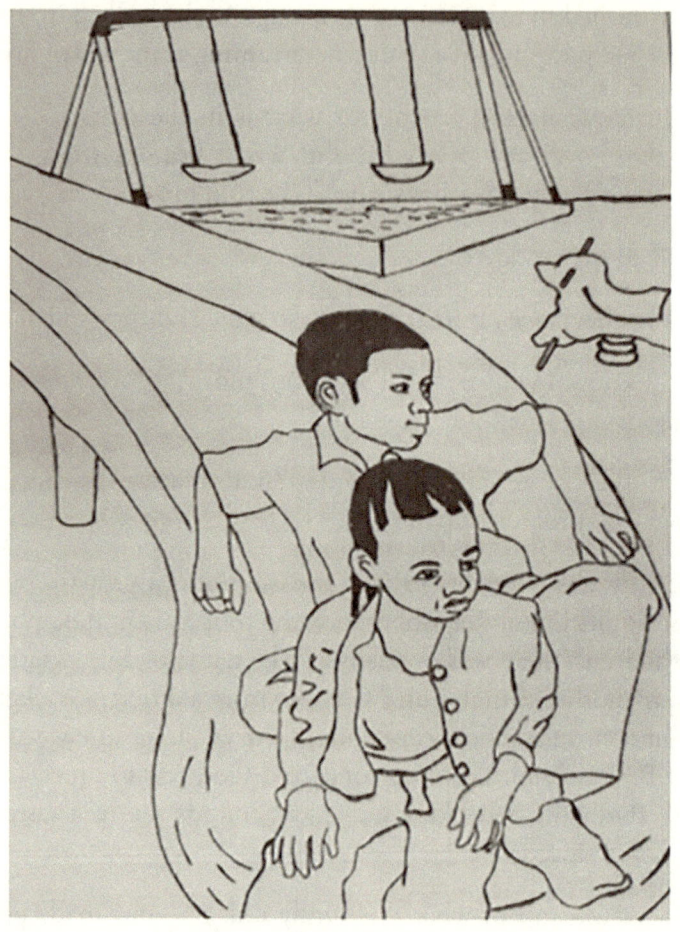

"A playground made with love"

They all showed us much love. And because we didn't have a car, our Aunt Gloria and Uncle David would take us on picnics along with their children. My first time seeing a blind person was when I met my Uncle David; it seems impossible that anyone could cheat him; he knew his money.

He knew a one-dollar bill from a twenty and he knew every coin. If a person tried walking up on him, he knew exactly who they were. He was a great uncle to us, and it was pleasurable just being around him and Aunt Gloria.

Aunt Gloria was another person who was known as a fighter too, and she didn't back down from anyone, boy or girl. Mom said that when they were growing up, she was considered a tomboy, and I realized that this came to me naturally, too.

One day, for some reason, Mom bought a car knowing that she didn't even know how to drive. Dad would drive it sometimes just to move it. But we used the hood for dancing. We weren't allowed to dance or play our music in the house. Therefore, whenever Mom was at work, the party was taken outside to the side of the house. It wasn't a secret any longer; when Mom got home from work, Grandma May told her everything we did.

We were already at the age where we didn't need a sitter. Since all our houses were surrounding one another's, the older adults could see everything that was going on with us. Mom didn't get upset with us; we respected her rules and did our music and dancing outside of the house. She also told us that she remembered being a child once, too.

CHAPTER 12

"An open door"

Even though I was getting older, there were some things that are going to remain the same. That next day, after we did our house chores, we walked to Grandma's house. All I wanted was to do my favorite thing, which was climbing and sitting up in that old Chinaberry tree in Grandma May and Uncle Pete's front yard, picking chinaberries for my puffer.

When we were younger, Uncle Pete and Bill showed us how to make puffer, and it was a joy ever since. Or we liked going under the house catching yak-key-. doodles. On that day the wind was blowing, and it felt so good just sitting there.

"Sitting in a world of my own"

As I sat there in my own little world, I noticed my brother Bill was talking to a boy, and I found out later that he was Bill's brother-in-law.

Bill tried to get me to come down to meet him. All I wanted to do was stay there in that tree. Playing at Grandma's house was always great, and that was my way of escaping.

By the time I came down, he was gone. It didn't matter to me, not one little bit. I couldn't figure out what was wrong with me as a child. It appears I could never fit in. Something was missing, yet I knew that there were some of my family members that seemed to care.

Uncle Troy and Uncle Wile were married guys and had children; they were Mom's other brothers. Uncle Wile was the shortest of Mom's brothers, and he was very nice. Going to his house was great because he was a preacher. He didn't come around as much, even though he only lived down the street from his sibling. He served in the military for a long time. He didn't seem as happy as he should be. Uncle Pete was in the military as well; they served their country with great pride.

Uncle Troy was a happy kind of man. He never mistreated any of us. He played with us, and it was a joy to be around him and Auntie. I also made extra money watching over his and Uncle Wile's children. Uncle Wile had a daughter by the name of Kim—my first cousin. Every time they asked me to babysit her and her siblings, she would always be the one that wouldn't listen to me.

That girl didn't listen or do anything I asked her. I had to show her who was in charge, so one day she realized that I was the one in charge, not her. Then only we were able to have fun together. After that, I didn't have any more problems with her.

Now Mom decided that it was time for us to move again. She found a house that was better than all the others.

This was the house that Uncle Troy and his family moved out from; this house had lights and plumbing but no indoor bathroom. We were moving up slowly, but I knew that we would get there someday. At this time, I started drawing the attention of boys my age, but I decided to protect myself and build up walls. I vowed not to allow anyone to come in. I had to protect my feelings.

When I was fifteen, my brother Bill decided that he and his wife were moving out of town. He asked Mom if it would be okay if I could help them pack. It was fine with her. After school, I walked to Bill's house. No one was at home. "*Well, I'll wait here for a little while; maybe they would be back shortly,*" I said to myself. As I waited, I noticed clothes hangers with white paper on them lying on the ground. I picked one up at a time and wrote little notes on them and hung them on the windows and doors.

The note read: *Next time, when you ask someone to come over and help pack, be home OK, Signed Jackie.* Just as I was about to hang my last note, Bill pulled up in a moving truck with his brother-in-law. I looked and thought, "*oh no that's the same boy Bill was talking to some months ago. Well, I'm not going in that house now for sure!*"

I stayed out for a while, walking around the backyard picking up pecans.

But he kept looking at me through the window. "*Why is he looking at me?*" I thought to myself.

"Jackie," Bill called. "Come here. I want to introduce you to someone."

As I walked in, I thought to myself, "*why does he want to introduce me to this boy? He is the ugliest person I have ever seen.*"

Walking into the house, I felt so nervous, because I wasn't sure what Bill was thinking about. But one thing I *did* know was that he would not do anything to hurt me., so, my nerves relaxed, and I looked at the boy and said, "Hi." At that time, Bill introduced us. "Jackie, this is Mason, and Mason, this is Jackie.

"*I guess he won't bite*"

He said hello and shook my hand. Afterward, I turned around and walked away.

I started helping my sister-in-law pack. It seemed like everywhere I went I felt his eyes were on me, but I continued helping Pam pack. I always enjoyed being around her. It made me very sad that they were going to move away soon. Pam seem as though she love me, and I loved her, my new big sister.

I helped for a few hours, then I had to leave and go home as my schoolwork was waiting. But that wasn't the end of Mason. About four days later, Bill came to our house just to check on Mom and us as well; but he also wanted to let us know that they decided not to move away after all.

"Hey Jackie, come here!" he called out to me.

"Hey, Bill what's up?" I said.

"Guess what girl?" he said to me.

"I don't know. What is it, Bill?"

"Girl, Mason likes you," he said with a smile on his face.

"Who is that?" I asked

"Girl, you know Mason-- my brother-in-law. He was at my house a few days ago."

"Ha! Are you kidding me? *That ugly* boy? I don't think so! Not me."

"Did you notice how he was looking at you? He made me laugh about something he said. "And what was that, Bill? What was so funny?"

"He said that you were the prettiest girl he had ever seen." "Oh yep, well, he is not the best-looking person I've ever seen."

"Jackie, he would be a great person for you. He's a hard worker. He's clean, and he wants something in life." "Really, and what is that?"

"You'll just have to see," said Bill.

"Okay, Bill, I will meet him."

"Well," I started to say, then Mom interrupted with, "Wait what? No Bill, she is not old enough to date anyone, she is only 15 years old. She must wait until she is 16, and not a day sooner."

"But Mom, this is a good person," Bill explained. "He is my brother-in- law. He is a good man. He is a hard worker and is very clean. Come, on just meet him, Mom, just meet him and you will see."

Since Mom trusted Bill, she said, "Ok, tell him to come by the house on Saturday to meet his dad and me and then we will see," said Mom.

Saturday was only two days away, but it seemed longer. About 1 pm that Saturday, there was a knock on the door. Mom opened it.

"Hello, are you Mrs. Jones?" said a voice.

"Yes, I am," said Mom.

"My name is Mason Robertson, your son Bill's brother-in-law."

"Come in," she replied.

As Mason walked in, Dad smiled. "Hi Slim, how are you, and why are you here?" Dad said in a very surprised tone.

"Oh, Matt, this is the young man that I told you about, Bill's brother-in-law," Mom said.

"What! So, your name is Mason? I never knew you by that name, I only knew you by the name of Slim," Dad said. "Have a seat."

"Thanks," Mason answered. He seemed more relaxed now that he was in the company of someone he knew. After some small talk, Mason sat back in his chair, and took a deep breath, "Well, Mr. and Mrs. Jones," he said. "I want to know: will you allow me to date your daughter, Jackie?"

Before Dad could answer Mom, asked him, "Well, young man, how old are you? Jackie is only 15 years old."

"I am 17 years old," Mason answered.

"You're what? Seventeen? You look so much older. Are you sure that you are not at least 21 years old?" Mom said with a surprised look on her face.

"No Ma'am, I'm only 17 years old," he answered.

"Ok," she replied.

"Mason, as my wife stated, Jackie is only 15 years old, and we weren't going to allow her to date until she is16. Son, are you ready to be responsible for what comes with dating?"

"Yes sir, I am," Mason replied with great confidence.

"What would you do if she gets pregnant? Are you going to walk away and leave her to deal with the child alone?"

"No sir, I will not! I may be seventeen but would not abandon her. I have a good job. I would do right by her."

They talked for a long time about responsibility, and Mason understood everything.

"Okay, Slim, I heard every word that you said. My wife and I will be back soon. We need to talk."

They walked out of the room. As they walked away, Mason looked at me and asked a question, "Jackie, what do you think they will say?"

"It will be okay. But I talked with Mom and she trusts Bill's opinion, besides, Dad knows you too."

As we were talking, Mom and Dad walked in. "Okay, you two young people, we will allow you to date, but you promise me, Slim, that you will not hit or mistreat my girl."

"I do promise, Sir!" said Mason.

Dad set the days and times that we were allowed to see one another. Mason agreed to everything, and this was the beginning of the rest of my life. At first, I didn't care that much about him, but that changed and changed fast. He treated me like a young lady. I never thought anyone would ever care so much about me. As time passed, my feelings began to change. Mason seemed to care, and he became my best friend. Wow, someone loves me, I thought. He made me feel so beautiful.

He treated me like a queen. I began to laugh and enjoy life, something I hadn't done in a very long time. Mason exposed me to a world I didn't know existed. At first, it was scary, but he made me feel safe. And nothing would ever hurt me again if he was around.

Because of my Christian upbringing, a lot of things he did that I didn't do or didn't understand, such as going to house parties, drinking, and smoking; this was Mason's world. Even though we were dating, my parents told him not to take me to any house parties or on boat rides. He took me to so many other places and we had so much fun; My life was great.

I started loving him more and more. There was a drive-in movie theater at the end of the main street in our neighborhood, which we were never allowed to go to. But Mason took me there, and it was so much joy to see-- Wow! The excitement in my life, because of this young man, was unreal, yet so real. We would talk and laugh for hours; it was fun getting to know one another. But even with that, there were times when I wanted to test our relationship to see how solid his commitment to me was.

I would say or act like I didn't want him around sometime. He didn't like that. "Jackie, why are you acting like that? You need to stop before Mason walks off and leaves you," said Jerome. Well, that night I almost lost him. I guess the way I was acting was too much for him to handle.

CHAPTER 13

"Boiling water can hurt"

Mason looked at me and said, "Jackie, I don't know what's wrong with you but it's over between us!" With those words, he walked out of the front door. "See, I told you! I am going to tell Momma about you when she gets home," Jerome added.

"I don't care! Tell her! Let him go! That's what he wanted to do in the first place."

I walked to the door and watched as Mason walked away. My heart started to ache, but I didn't say a word. I turned around and went to my bedroom stretched out on my bed and fell asleep knowing how I acted was wrong, and it made me so sad inside. The next morning, waking up to the sound of the rooster crowing, I realized what I did.

I jumped up and got dressed and ran to Grandma's house to call Mason and ask him to please forgive me for acting so foolish. And it was just in time; my phone call was right on schedule. Mason had packed his bags and was about to move to Washington DC with his sister.

"Girl, your timing was good, because after last night, I said I wasn't staying here any longer. That was going to be the first and last time that I care for someone and let them hurt my feelings like that," said Mason.

That day I grew up and stopped playing childish games. I realized that Mason really cared for me. That day I was his and he was mine. I loved this man day by day. He became the air that I breathed, and he was my heartbeat. He was my teacher, my friend, my spirit, my world. Mason showed me so much love, I didn't know how to deal with it. So, I finally opened up about all my pains and fears to him.

As I talked, he embraced me with such care and my heart just melted. "Jackie, I am so sorry that you had to deal with so much pain, but I want you to know that I will never, ever hurt you like that." After that day, his every wish was my pleasurable demand for me.

Some of the family members seemed to hate the idea that someone thought I was a beautiful person. My first cousin who worked with Mason, walked over to my house to talk to me. Now that wasn't unusual. But what he said was, "Hey cuz, we are family, and we must look out for each other. I heard that you are now dating Mason. Watch out because he may be only dating you for what he can get."

"Okay, thanks," I responded. I knew Mason liked to drink and party, and he was still seeing other ladies that partied as he did. But, that's okay: *He is my life now, and my sail is up and the wind has already started blowing; only God can guide it in the right direction. To me, God is my light during the dark times. And he is the only one that knows my destiny where I am and where I am going.*

Dating was an experience that wasn't a regular part of my world; it was fun going places I'd never been before and trying new things. Wow! Life was so good that I forgot all about the pains of life. Mason was my best friend, my life, and my world.

There was an aunt of mine that said to me, "Jackie; that boy is not going to stay with you. He is too good-looking, and he is just using you for what he can get. Give it six months and it will be over; you watch and see."

There were a few of my cousins that couldn't wait to tell me what he was doing, even my friends in the neighborhood told me that they were going to take him from me.

Wow! What kind of friends and family were these? They tried everything in the book to break us up, but it didn't work. Each time,

Mason would tell me that what they were trying to do was to come between us. Our relationship grew. The man I thought was so ugly was looking mighty good to me now. He treated me like a queen. He was my teacher of life and everything else.

I was trying to be a big girl and stop fighting, but sometimes I was pushed too far. One day after high school, while I was getting off the bus, we all were walking home, and my very best friend was talking about my sister Step and her brother. By this time, Step had a son by my best friend's brother. Ann wanted to show off in front of all our friends. I warned her to stop, but she wouldn't. So I picked up a stick and told her to knock it out of my hands.

She did it and the fight was on. I won again. For us to be best friends we were always fighting one another. I won every time; maybe that was one reason we fought so much. She was hoping one day she may beat me; now that would be a day. After it was over, I was thinking that was the end of that.

The next morning after getting off the school bus, my cousin Tony and I were walking toward the school building; I heard someone call my name. I turned around to see who it was; to my surprise, it was Ann and about twenty other schoolmates. "Jackie, we are going to finish this now," she said. Ann kept talking about my sister again in front of everyone.

I told her to stop talking about my sister. The more she talked, the more anger was setting in, and it was coming on fast. Tony noticed it. "Jackie, come on, it is not worth it; Walk away from her!" said Tony. I was trying to do as he said, but as I turned my back to walk away, Ann caught me by my hair. That's what I was waiting— for her to touch me first.

I threw my books on the ground, and the next thing I knew I was sitting in the principal's office. I sat there looking around; wondering where Ann was. About fifteen minutes later she walked in with the school nurse. I looked at her and I almost didn't recognize her. Her face was covered with bandages, and blood was all over her shirt.

We had to sit there until someone picked us up. The principal talked to us about fighting; I tried to tell him that I didn't start it, but he didn't want to hear anything from either of us. Mom had to leave work to catch the bus and come get me from school. Now, that hurts me more than anything, seeing how this lady worked so hard to keep things together; and here I was, acting like a person with no sense. I realized that I shouldn't allow anyone to bring me down to their level. That was the last time I fought anyone else.

Over a year of our courtship, I found myself sleeping more than usual. Mom noticed it as well. I didn't think much of it until Mom called me into her room. "Jackie, come here. Let's talk. How are you feeling? I have been noticing you for about two months now. You are sleeping a lot and eating things I have never seen you eat before."

"I am fine. There isn't anything wrong with me Mom," I responded.

"Well, we need to make sure. Tomorrow, I will take you to the doctor."

"Mom, I am not sick."

"Maybe not, but I believe that you are pregnant," she said. Now *those* words were very frightening to me.

The next morning, Mom took me to the doctor as she said she would, and the report was true. I was pregnant. "Jackie, I will have to tell your dad about this, but it will be all right. Now you need to talk to Mason," she told me.

"Okay, Mom. I will. He's coming over tonight."

Mom told Dad and he became very upset. The main thing they talked to us about, had finally happened.

Dad yelled at me and said some things that cut to my heart. Then the fear of Mason walking away and leaving me was the same feeling I believe my mother had when Matt walked away and left her. So maybe Dad was so upset because he knew Mason's lifestyle, and he didn't want me to travel the same road as Mom and my sister. At 7:00 P.M., there was a knock at the door; it was Mason.

When he walked in, he knew something was wrong. He looked at me and raised his shoulders as if to say, "Jackie what's wrong?"

"Slim, I need to talk with you. Now!" Dad said to Mason. They walked outside to talk. I thought that I was going to hear a lot of yelling, but I didn't; laughing is what I heard. About twenty minutes later, they were back inside.

"Jackie, come on. Let's go for a ride," Mason said. If you were to look at Mason, you would think that he was much older than he really was. His maturity level was far beyond his actual age. As we walked, holding hands, he said to me, "Jackie, you know what, what your dad said to me didn't surprise me."

"I knew something was wrong because I found myself sleeping a lot. And my mom asked me if you were in a family way." "What did you say?" I asked him.

"I told her that I didn't think so. But I knew somehow, But I see that she knew something that I didn't know. So, Mason, what is next? Are you going to walk away like everyone said you would?" I asked him.

To my surprise, and to shock everyone else, he didn't. Instead, he asked me to become his wife. That almost blew me away.

My body was changing fast, and I didn't understand what was happening

Mason brought me some books to read and then he explained everything to me in- depth.

After he explained about childbirth, I was more terrified than ever. "Jackie, you will be okay; I am not going anywhere," he assured me.

One Sunday morning, I woke up in so much pain that I called out to mom. After checking on me, she told Jerome to call Mason. He came in a hurry to see what was going on with me.

After eighteen hours of labor, Mason Jr. was finally born. Five months later, we were married. At this time, I was seventeen and

Mason was nineteen. But even though he is so young, he already knew so much about life, and he always acted older than he was. He told me that he got his first job at the age of eight and was working ever since. Finally, the day came for us to get married, and I was so happy to be marrying my very best friend in the world.

By this time, Mom and Dad had moved into a beautiful house that sat on a hill: It had an indoor bathroom, which for us was the first time having this luxury. We had a washer, running water, everything. Now, this is living! I would go in the bathroom just to flush the toilet and see how it worked. Mom and Step were working so hard to get things together. The house looked great! We had a beautiful house wedding. Uncle Pete married us; Lots of friends and family showed up.

It was time for me and Dad to take that walk down the aisle; but it wasn't an aisle. It was from the back of the house to the living room in the front of the house. As Dad was walking to give me away, he ran. "Slow down, Dad, slow down.

What's the hurry?" I asked.

He said, "Come on, girl, it looks like it's going to rain!"

After the wedding, we were about to leave, and my dad packed his bags and said he was going with us. "Come on Mason, where are we going?" Dad said. Mason said, "You can't go with us", said Mason. Dad said, "Why not? This is my daughter."

He carried on as though he was serious about what he was saying. Mom said, "Matt, what is wrong with you? You can't go with them."

Finally, Dad realized that he wasn't going with us, so he walked away and sat on his favorite chair in the living room; but here is something that mom told me, that on their wedding day that happened to Mom when she and Dad were married. They didn't have a place to stay. So, here I am walking down that same path, but a door was opened to us. We stayed one night with Mom and Dad. Later, we moved in with Mason's mother and father.

"My dream came true"

CHAPTER 14

"The unknown"

We stayed there until Mason felt it was time to leave, but where would we go? Mason talked to Bill and Pam about staying with them until we found a place to stay. They were more than happy for us to stay with them, so Mason, Mason Jr. and I moved in. Pam helped me with more cooking lessons, and it was so much fun being with her.

About three weeks later, I found an apartment in the newspaper. It was $37.50 for rent. Pam took me to check it out and it was a mess with roaches and rats, but I liked it. When Mason came home, he checked it out himself. "Oh Jackie, it's a mess! But it has potential, and with a lot of hard work, we can do it," he said.

We signed the lease and worked for three weeks on that three-room apartment. Finally, it was ready, and we moved in. Now we were a family with our very own place to live in.

"It was home to us"

But then I took sick; I was swelling up all the time. It was like I was in an ant bed all the time. I was having an allergic reaction to something, but to what? Mason took me to the emergency room, and they gave me so many shots. The doctor didn't know what was causing me to break out. The next day I was sitting on our bed and broke out crying. "What is wrong, honey?" Mason asked in such a caring voice.

"I am allergic to you, Mason!" I cried, as I tried to get each word out. "No, you are not; we will find out what it is soon; don't worry."

But my lips looked like a truck had run over them. Later, we found out that I had an allergic reaction to a blanket that he brought home from his job that was on our bed. I was so happy about finding that out.

One night, Mason's sister Earnestine from Texas came to visit us; she asked if she could stay the night and we both agreed.

Things were going great; after we all talked, we settled down for a good night's sleep. At about 3 am that morning, there was a scream. "Oh my god, Help! Mason, come here now!" his sister yelled.

"What is wrong Earnestine?" asked Mason.

"Mason, two rats were dancing in the middle of the floor; I thought that they were going to jump on me!" said Earnestine in a panicky voice.

Mason left the light on for his sister to feel safe.

Earnestine got up later that morning, looking around to see if the rats were gone and they were. "Earnestine, what is all that on the floor?" asked Mason.

"That is my body powder; I was trying to scare them off," she replied. She left that morning and never stayed another night with us.

There was always something going on upstairs with the couple that lived there. It seemed like they fought every night. Mason grew up with them, therefore he knew them well. One night, we were watching television and there was a knock at the door. Mason answered it; The young lady was standing there crying with black eyes and nothing on. Her husband had beaten her, torn off her clothes, and kicked her out of the apartment.

We felt so sorry for her that I took a blanket and covered her up and that night she slept on our sofa. The next morning, they were together again as if nothing had happened.

We had no idea what was about to happen in our lives. Sometimes, working for a moving company, Mason was able to get ahold of some small, nice things. Not big, but God was about to close that chapter of his life.

One night, Mom asked us to go to a "revival" at her church. There was a preacher from up north who was the revivalist. This was one of the same preachers that I had seen as a child.

The service was great and then there was a prayer line called. Mom told us to go for prayer and we did. We both gave our hearts to the Lord that night. The interesting thing was that the preacher said, "Go and sin no more." But the kicker was that he *also* said, "He that steals, steal no more."

Mason took the words just as it was. The next morning, he took his very nice car, his favorite car, back from where he got it. And everything that was in the apartment that wasn't ours, was set aside.

I looked through the window as the trash collectors had a field day.

"What a deal"

That weekend, we went shopping for whatever we needed. After all that shopping, I was so tired that I went to the bathroom to take a bath. I started yelling, "Mason! Mason! AH! AH! My God! There's a rat in the bathtub!" Mason ran and he laughed so hard.

He picked it up by the tail and threw it out the back door. He also cleaned the bathtub! I wouldn't take a bath until he did. I was always on my guard looking out. Mason put traps around the house and caught a few. My baby was in the house, and I didn't want anything to happen to him.

The holidays were approaching. First, Thanksgiving, and then Christmas. It was our first holiday together as a family and I wanted to make it special.

All of us always met at Mom's house for dinner now that her family was getting bigger. Now that Thanksgiving was here, I wanted to cook a turkey for my baby that he could eat later. I never did this before, so this would be my first time. Everything was set; the oven was ready. I washed the turkey well, seasoned it, put it in the bag, and then placed it in the oven. I cooked everything else for about four hours, and then the turkey was ready. "It smells so good, and everything looks great Jackie," said Mason.

We sat down to enjoy our small Thanksgiving meal before going to Mom's house. I had so much fun cooking it. After the blessing, Mason cut the turkey, "Jackie! You forgot to take the bag out of the turkey!"

"What bag?'

He lifted it up. "See this bag?"

"I'm so sorry I didn't know they put that in there," I answered. To this day we still laugh about my first turkey. It didn't go to waste; my cousin came around and took it home.

The next holiday was Christmas; we were so excited. Mason went to get a tree for our house. It was a pine tree, he cut the top off, shaped it up like a round boxwood hedge, and set it in a big container of dirt. We decorated it with Christmas lights. It was bent over because the bulbs were too heavy for the poor tree; it was a funny-looking tree, but it was our first tree. We were young and having fun together.

Two months later, Mason Jr. turned a year old, and I was expecting another baby. Mason said that we needed a bigger place. When we were able, we found another apartment. The new one was so much bigger than the first one. And this house had a big pecan tree in the backyard. What made it even better was that Mom, Tim, and Katrina moved in next door, and Dad as well. During this time, my taste buds were so crazy. My favorite snack was the wooden jelly between the pecans-- it tasted so good to me.

Nine months later, Jay was born, but he couldn't come home with me. He stayed in the hospital for three weeks because of Jaundice. My blood is type O with Rh negative, and Jay was not. Therefore, Bilirubin levels in my baby were a little higher after birth. High levels of Bilirubin in the body can cause the skin to look yellow, this is called Jaundice.

It seemed like the days were moving so slowly. Every day I was at the hospital with my baby. Finally, I was able to bring Jay home with me. We were all so happy.

"Jackie, do you notice anything?" asked Mason.

"Notice what? I don't know what you are talking about."

"Do you remember when we were talking about marriage? We both said that we wanted two boys and two girls and that we wanted the boys to be older than the girls. Well, look. We have our boys. We also said that we wanted a house with a big Oak tree in the front yard and a fence around the house. Watch and see what is happening," Mason said with a proud look on his face.

"You are so right, Mason! I didn't think about that. My god!"

Now that we are all home, things could fall into place. I couldn't go to church yet, but it wouldn't be that long. Mason Jr. was enjoying being a big brother to his new baby brother.

God was blessing us so wonderfully. Being next to Mom made me feel safe and I know that she will be there to help me with my second baby like she did with Mason Jr. Jay was growing and moving fast. Mom said to me, "Jackie, Jay is moving mighty fast. Are you alright?"

"Yes Ma'am, I am good," I answered.

The boys were taking a nap, Mason and I went to the backyard to pick up some pecans when I heard some noise up in the tree. I looked up to see what it was, and Pigeon feces got into my mouth.

"Just nasty"

Mason laughed so hard that tears rolled down his face. I could not do enough to get that taste out of my mouth. "Girl, I don't want to kiss you for a long time!" Mason said as he laughed. It was on my mind for years afterward. The next time I went to the backyard, I didn't look up no matter how much noise I heard.

CHAPTER 15

"Bullseye"

The stars were shining so brightly this night, as Mason and I sat on the porch playing with our boys. Tim and Katrina came over to play with Mason Jr. then Jerome called out to me. "Jackie! Come here, something is wrong with Mom!" We jumped up and ran next door to see what was wrong. When we walked in, Mom was having a very hard time breathing. That was so scary. I think she thought that she was going to die that night.

"Jackie, call the ambulance now, and don't worry baby, I will be alright. I need you to promise me that you will look after your brother and sister for me." I had never seen her like this before and I didn't know what to do. She was wheezing badly and had severe shortness of breath. She was speaking very slowly that she was having a very bad asthma attack.

"Mom what can I do?"

Jerome called for the ambulance and stayed by Mom's side, praying for her. By the time the ambulance got there, she was feeling better. Praise the Lord! Though they kept her in the hospital for a week to get mucus off her lungs.

Right after Mom came home from the hospital, Dad developed tuberculosis. They sent him to a hospital in Augusta, Georgia, where they kept him for months. When he came home, he didn't look the same. He had gained weight, and his skin had cleared up.

Jay was now three months old, and my husband said it was time to get a bigger place. So, I went looking and I found myself in an area not too far from where we grew up. I didn't know that they were building new homes back there. I noticed a vacant lot. I told my mom that I wanted that lot for our new home. We prayed and our pastor prayed for us as well.

My husband was up for a pay raise on his job, but for some reason, he didn't get it. After going through the process, we were approved for our new home

"The favor of God is always a blessing"

The company told us that if my husband had made a dime more, we wouldn't have been approved. After we were approved, my husband's raise came through. God was on the plan the whole time. He knew how to work things out in our favor. My mother-in-law helped me pick out the interior color and the bricks for the new house.

Afterward, my husband had to put his final approval on our choices, and he liked them all. Jay was six months old when we moved into our brand-new home. We had our new home dedicated to the Lord. The saints from the church came out and rejoiced with us.

Nine months after we moved in, we had our first baby girl. Her godfather wanted to give her a name I didn't like, so I named her Latasha. Latasha had same jaundice that Jay had. But she had serious complications and putting her under those special blue lights didn't help her at all. The doctors told my husband and me that they were going to do a partial transfusion to see if it would help our baby girl.

I cried so hard until my blood pressure went so high and they gave me something to calm me down. There were people calling the hospital telling me that Latasha was sick because I didn't name her what her godfather wanted. I was so upset; here is my baby, fighting for her life, and instead of them praying, they were adding more stress-- it was something I didn't need.

The doctors tried the partial transfusion, and it didn't work. They said she was in a serious condition and they would have to do a total fresh blood replacement. My mind went back to the time when my baby brother Mark died, and the pain Mom went through. My heart began to ache more. I almost knew how Mom felt.

The tears couldn't stop falling and my husband did everything he could to comfort me. Holding me close was a great help. They told us the risk, but we knew she was in God's hands and all we had to do was trust Him. During this time, my husband and I talked about Latasha's name; we were young and afraid of losing our baby, so we decided to change her name to Christiania Lee, the name her godfather wanted. He was an old deacon of the church.

The transfusion seemed to be working for Christiania Lee; We were so blessed and happy in God's favor. I came home without my baby; she had to stay in the hospital for two long months. When the time was up, I couldn't drive a car yet, so our next-door neighbor took me to pick up my baby girl. What a joy it was to be able to hold my child in my arms!

Mom was right there with the grits, liver, and brown gravy. Each time Step and I had a baby, that was what she gave us to eat. By now, Step had three boys and I had two boys and a girl. I was enjoying my family. After a month passed, I was back in church. We believed everything our leader said, and if they said it was wrong, we didn't do it. I thank God for that because He has seen us through a lot of hard times.

I couldn't understand some things, especially when it comes to being fruitful and multiplying; I knew that was what the word of God said, but now my faith was being tested again. My baby girl was only three months old, and I was with a child again. I cried so hard and prayed every day, I wasn't sure whether I was right or wrong, but I told the Lord and I meant it with all my heart that I didn't want another child, NOT NOW!

My husband came home each day for weeks asking me if I was okay. I said, "Things are okay."

This was making me so sad. Here I was, trying to take care of three children, the house, and my husband. There was a fight going on within me. I fought with everything in me to keep from going into a state of depression. I didn't say a word to anyone, not even my husband, but there was one person that knew. How they knew, I didn't know.

One day I was over at Mom and Dad's house, sitting and talking with Mama. Dad walked in and sat during our conversation. He interrupted me and told me to stand up. *Okay, what is it now?* I was thinking to myself.

"Come here," he said. He stood in front of me, looking at my throat. "Jackie, you are with a child," he told me. "Do you want to know how I know this?"

"Yes sir," I answered.

"Go in the room and bring me my mirror on the dresser." I did as I was told; I knew that I was, but I hadn't told anyone; I kept it to myself.

As I walked back in with the mirror he said, "Now put it to your throat." So, I did. He pointed to the bottom and said, "There are two heartbeats-- yours and the child." The only thing I said then was, "Oh, my." I had never seen such a thing before. I went home and prayed and fasted more. It looked as if I was going to have this baby after all. So, I made up my mind that this must be God's will.

I decided to stop fasting and praying about this baby. One evening during my daily chores, I became very sick. The pain was so bad I thought that I was dying. My husband took me to the emergency room. At first, they didn't know what the problem was.

The pain wasn't lightening up by any means. They finally told me that I had a very bad bladder infection. I was given three prescriptions and sent home. The pain got even worse, and the pills weren't helping. The next day, which was a Monday morning, my husband didn't go to work. He didn't want to leave me but I insisted that I was feeling much better, and Mom would be there to watch the children, and me as well.

About an hour before he walked out of the door, the phone rang; it was Mom telling me that she had to go to work. Grandma May would come over to help until Mason came home from work, but he had to pick her up from the house. Sure enough, she was ready when he picked her up. She prayed for me, and the pills had me sleeping mostly all day. After a few hours, Mason was back home. His boss told him that he can left early since I was sick. He and the children took Grandma May home.

While he was gone, the pain woke me out of my sleep. I had to go to the bathroom. I couldn't walk, so I got on my hands and knees, and crawled.

Once I made it to the restroom, I pulled myself up on the sink. Just as I sat on the commode, I passed something that scared me, so I screamed out in pain and fear, but no one was there to help me. I picked it up and wrapped it in a bath towel; I had no idea what was going on or what was it that I had passed. When Mason returned, I was on the bathroom floor.

He helped me to the bed, and I showed him what was in the towel. Even though that happened, the pain was still there. He decided to take me back to the emergency room. The doctor told us that they still didn't know what was wrong; the only thing that they had seen was a bladder infection.

Mason picked up the towel and showed the doctor what was in it. Right away they knew what had happened. "Okay, I see now, Mrs. Robertson. It looks like you had a miscarriage," said the doctor that was in charge.

"A what?" asked Mason.

The doctor explained what it was. He also told us that I would need to have a *dilation and curettage*, known as a D & C, immediately.

"And because your wife has an Rh-negative blood type, I will have to give her a shot of Rh immune globulin. This will prevent Rh sensitization. Someday, you both may want to try again," said the doctor.

The next morning the D & C was performed, and I returned home after staying in the hospital for two days. God knew my heart's desire, so I can't say I lost the baby because God answered my prayer. From what the doctor said, my body wasn't strong enough to carry another baby so soon. He also told us that I shouldn't have any more children, because if I did, the baby or I may not live. After a few days, I was my old self again.

CHAPTER 16

"The smell of success"

Serving my husband was more than a joy to me. There was a time when we only had one car. He cared so much for the family, that he made sure that the car was just at home with me and the children. In the morning, I would take him to work; and in the evening, I would pick him up with the children. Sometimes, he would drive his Mack eighteen-wheeler truck home. He was a very hard worker.

After driving trucks for so many years, he wanted to try something new that paid more money, so he got a job that build and repair lift stations. The money was better, but the job wasn't. He would always come home smelling like sewage. Before he walked into the house, he would have to change his clothes in the washroom. His bath water was always waiting for him, and afterward, his dinner was served. He worked this job for three long years.

The smell was so bad it had gotten to his skin. So after three years, he left that job and returned to the road driving a tractor and trailer. Mom would watch the children for us since they were already much older. Therefore, I would be able to travel with him on the road sometimes, and that was so much fun. Seeing other places was very exciting for me. I recall the first time he ever took me up North with him and we stopped South of the border. "Oh, Mason. Look! We are in Mexico." I said with a big smile on my face.

"No baby, we are not in Mexico. We are just at the border that separates the South from the North." He looked at me with a soothing smile on his face.

We were enjoying being on the road together. He taught me how to take inventory along with so many other important and interesting skills. Our lives were so good that some people said I was living in a fairytale, and that someday my fairytale world would come crashing on me. Maybe so, but for now we are very happy and enjoying our family.

The teachings that we were getting from all the ministers at church were all about marriage, and we were taking it in. Some people can't stand to see young people happy. My mom had to live a life of unhappiness and she had to work with the hand that was dealt to her. Mom gave me her strength; I have seen it firsthand.

My husband said that his mom and dad fought as well. We promised one another that we would not let our children get into our problems. We didn't want to live our life that way. Things were going great: the money was coming, and the bills were getting paid. But then, my husband's company came up with an idea to put all the drivers on commission pay. At first, it was great, and the money was looking good. We were able to get some of the things that we needed. Mason Jr. and Jay were older now therefore, my husband would take them with him on the road. They enjoyed riding in that big truck with their daddy.

But then the paychecks became less and less. Paying the bills and getting food for the house was getting harder and harder. Mason said the most important thing to him was keeping a roof over his family's head, even if we had to go on without water, lights, or gas. It came to that point so many times. There were times when we didn't even have any food in the house.

I would take the children to Mom's house, and she would make sure they ate something. She would also fix something for Mason and me to eat. One thing is for sure, we could always depend on Mom. In so many ways, my life was almost like the mirror image of Mom's life. I can also recall feeding my family, and then I would eat the remaining rice crust that was left in the pot for my dinner.

My husband worked so hard to get more long – distance trips. But because of the gas surplus he brought home more zero checks than he cared to. We kept all this to ourselves; even though mom would help us out she had no idea how bad things really were.

One day sitting around the house the doorbell rang; to my surprise it was his mom stopping by to check on us. She asked for a glass of cold water, as I was headed toward the refrigerator to get it, she said to me, which I thought was strange; "No, Jackie, I will get it myself." Well, that is when she noticed that our refrigerator was empty.

She then gave me a few dollars to buy something for dinner that night. When Mason came home from work, he was so surprised and asked where I got the money to buy food with. I told him; but he wasn't happy about that at all. Mason is a very proud man. He didn't want anyone to know about our money issues, especially his mom.

That next day he decided to leave the truck-driving job once again, and return to that job he hated, even though it made him sick at times; but the pay was so much better. He said that he would have to endure the suffering until something better came along. He worked this job for four long years.

Things at home were getting better. But someone was missing, that one baby girl that we always wanted. Currently, we have two boys and one girl. Our dream family was two boys and two girls. The boys are the oldest, that's on schedule, now one more girl is needed.

I was somewhat afraid to go back before the Lord and on behalf of another child. But eventually we did. We also asked our pastor to pray for and with us. One thing that we knew, no matter what the doctor said; GOD WAS THE ONE THAT WILL MAKE THE FINAL DECISION.

Well, it looked as if God was not going to answer our prayer request. But our leaders told us that whenever we go before God for something, whatever it is, leave it at the feet of the cross and walk away. So that is what we did-- trusting God to answer it. I decided, *if we don't get the answer we want, then it's not for us. Contentment is the key now; there is nothing else to do but trust God.*

That day after church, we decided to take the family for a ride in the country to see the horses. The excitement on their faces was worth the trip. Afterward, we went to the ice cream parlor; we were enjoying every moment of their childhood.

They had their share of dogs, but there was one pet that Mason Jr. had. This pet was a baby chick that he loved so dearly. But it grew so big that my husband told him that he would have to take it over to his father's house because we didn't have a place for it to stay.

MJ (Mason Jr.) trusted his grandfather to keep his word and not cook his pet. It seemed like every weekend MJ wanted to go and check on his pet, so my husband supported him by taking him. One Sunday after church, we were invited for dinner at Mason's parent's house (Mr. Jonathan & Mrs. Linda Brown). Guess what we had for dinner? Yes, fried chicken! MJ looked at his plate and burst out crying, tears were rolling down his face.

"What is wrong with you, MJ?" asked Mr. Jonathan. "Granddaddy, you killed my pet chicken!" He was crying and trying to get each word out as he spoke. "You... you... you *promised* me that you weren't going to kill it."

"No, no, this is not your pet. He is outside. Go look, you will see him," Mr. Jonathan replied in a calm voice. MJ jumped up from the table and ran outside to check on his pet. He was so pleased to see it was still there.

But that didn't last long. About a month later, MJ asked his father to take him to check on his pet. As his dad pulled up in the car; MJ ran to check, but this time it was gone. Mrs. Linda cooked the wrong chicken, and they were sitting down to eat it at that time. My little man cried for two long days. It was a long time before he ate chicken again, but eventually, he got over it.

My mom was always in my life; she helped me with my family when needed.

But there was, and will always be, a wall between my dad and me. I have such a hard time forgiving him for what he did—not only to me but to my whole family as well. I think at some point, he knew how unhappy we were with him. Therefore, he tried very hard to amend his way with all his grandchildren. They were the joy of his life, it seemed. It reminded me of us sometimes, as children, showing us off to his friends. But what was different was, they were able to keep and spend the money they got.

The heart is real; without it, there is no life. You see me, but you don't see it.

There is always something concealed in the dark because things are not always what they seem. A few years later, something else happened that made me wonder,*am I here or there?*

The End

A CANDLE BENEATH MY BED/ A HIDDEN HEART

A Hidden Heart continues the story of Jacqueline (aka Jackie) Jones' memories as a young girl facing life's hardship from book one (A Candle Beneath My Bed/ Betrayal). This is an electrifying page-turner- The young girl in this book is weak and vulnerable; well so people think.

There are some suspicious activities that are going around in the families and schools. Jackie is a warrior; she just doesn't know it yet.

See how Jackie comes to grips with everything that was happening in her life and around her. Sometimes you will never know the fright that is in a person until their back is against the wall.

Sandra Delores (Scott) Johnson is a native of Savannah, Ga. She was born to the late Mr. Joseph and Mrs. Rosa Lee Scott. She is the 4th child of 8 siblings. She has been married to the love of her life Louis Johnson Sr. for over 51 years. To their reunion, four children were born two boys and two girls. She is a wife, mother, grandmother, great-grandmother, sister, and friend.

She received a degree in early childhood from Savannah Vocational Technical School. She loves working with the youth. She was the founder of Y.A.W.T. , an outreach program that started in 1997.

She earned an Honor Bachelor's degree in Biblical Studies and is working on her master's degree in Christian Theology.

She is now serving as the 2nd Vice President of the Georgia State Women in ministry department. She enjoys writing and working with the youth, as well as with adult women. She is the Elect Lady of her church, where she serves as the President of the women's department, teaches bible study, and works with the youth, just to name a few.

www.ingramcontent.com/pod-product-compliance
Lightning Source LLC
Chambersburg PA
CBHW030316130626
46549CB00002B/886